My Life Is a War

Voices of Traumatized
Palestinian Children
under Israeli Occupation

by
Dr. Iman Farajallah

Sumud LCC

Paperback
ISBN: 979-8-218-39951-1

Subjects:
Psychology | Palestine | Trauma
Children | Healing |

First English edition.
Includes biographical references and appendices.
Text copy edited by Caitlin Dwyer
Book designed and typeset by Elipse Productions.

First Published in the United States of America

Contents

Preface

For over seven decades, the young inhabitants of Palestine have endured the relentless burden of escalating war-related traumas as a consequence of enduring and protracted conflicts with Israeli occupation. Palestinian children have been subjected to peril and violence on a scale that has, regrettably, given rise to a marginalized social stratum within their society. It is within this adversity that our research has found its purpose, which is deeply rooted in the calling to illuminate the profound psychological repercussions wrought by war.

Through our research, we undertake a comprehensive exploration of the multifaceted aspects surrounding the harrowing experiences of war and post-war trauma among children, with a particular focus on the children of Palestine. In the pages that follow, we shall embark on a journey into the lives of Palestinian children who have witnessed the cruelty of Israeli occupation. Our objective is twofold: to provide a depiction of their experiences and to shed light on the ongoing efforts and potential global interventions aimed at mitigating this human tragedy. In so doing, we appeal to empathy for addressing this issue, not merely as a regional concern, but as a testament to the collective humanity that binds us all.

Dr. Iman Farajallah

Dedication

I dedicate this work to the memory of my mother,
Nadira, and my brother, Fakri.
To my nephews Hussain and Muhammad,
and all my family members and all Palestinians who
were killed by the Israeli occupation.
You are not a number, and you are not forgotten.

To my father, Ibrahim, and my siblings.

To my children, Abedallah, Bayah, and Abedalrahman,
who have been my great support and inspiration.

Without my family's love, sacrifices, and support,
this work would never have been written.

To all children living in war zones and the children
of Palestine, especially the children of Gaza.

To all the individuals who have encouraged and supported
me throughout the years of researching and writing this work.

Thank you!

Acknowledgments

Working on this project had a big impact on me. I would like to acknowledge all those who have helped me and supported me in conducting this research. I am deeply indebted to the Gaza Community Mental Health Programme (GCMHP) for their support and help with this research. I would like to thank the staff of GCMHP, particularly Dr. Yasser Abu Jamei and psychologist Hassan Zeyada.

I owe a great debt of gratitude to all participants in this study who opened their hearts and shared their stories despite the painful memories. I am thankful to everyone who helped me conduct this research, particularly Dr. Sami Owaida, Dr. Kamal Qadih, Kifah Qadih, and Bilal Eid. Finally, I would like to express my deepest appreciation to my friends Tanya Brauer and Lotfi ben Yedder for their infinite support.

Thank you —you are ALL amazing and special to me.

Foreword

I would argue that we could and should all agree that children shouldn't be the ones paying the price when we adults fight. Unfortunately, that is not usually the case. It seems that manmade trauma is here to stay, and that we will continue to play catchup with the trauma story that is always one step ahead of us. Many adults pass their distorted trauma narrative to their children, risking trans-generational transmission of trauma. An ugly and heavy inheritance and legacy indeed. Many children in war-torn countries and areas of armed conflict never live a normal childhood. They miss out on two of their very basic needs and core beliefs, to believe that the world is a safe place and that adults can be trusted. Children of trauma who don't have the words to tell their story might speak up behaviorally. They might lash out or shut down. When children don't feel heard, they might scream louder or lose their voice. When they don't feel seen, they might "act out" or turn invisible. And when they don't trust adults to fulfill their needs, they might try to meet their own needs or deny they have any. The world can be a very dark and ugly place for children of trauma. It is our moral duty and ethical obligation to bring safety, hope, light, and beauty back to lives shattered by our own acts of ignorance, arrogance, hate, bigotry, dehumanizing, and othering. Dr. Iman Farajallah in this powerful manifesto has forced us to look at our own humanity and bear witness to the invisible wounds of the Palestinian children. Iman's focus on resilience, the human spirit, and the need to keep children away from this miss is necessary and admirable.

Dr. Omar Reda
author of *The Wounded Healer*

Introduction: A Traumatized Nation

An emergent body of scholarly research underscores the distressing national calamity unfolding before our eyes, casting a spotlight on the trauma endured by the children of Palestine, who daily grapple with war as a fixture in their lives. Numerous scholarly investigations have illuminated the grave psychological effects afflicting these young people. Regrettably, there has been inadequacy in addressing the profound psychological wounds inflicted by ceaseless political violence. As the ramifications of this crisis surface, the global community has begun to bear witness to the erosion of an entire cultural fabric and the cumulative and potentially irreparable psychological scars borne by these innocent children.

This book examines pivotal milestones in the psychological analysis and comprehension of the circumstances thrust upon these children, seeking to imbue these experiences with meaning and understanding. The keen aspiration here is that we draw lessons from these distressing events and respond with every resource at our disposal to extend solace, protection, and support to these children, regardless of whether their symptoms manifest in Palestine or closer to home. We strive to shield children from the ravages of trauma and to foster an environment where they may thrive.

This study explores the profound psychological impacts stemming from childhood trauma against the backdrop of war. Specifically, the investigation centers on the unique experiences of Palestinian children who endured the effects of the Israeli conflicts, with a particular emphasis on the 2014 war in Gaza. The objectives of this inquiry are to describe the trauma experienced by Palestinian children of Gaza during the Israeli war in the Gaza Strip in 2014, and to delve into the essential role of meaning-making in the process of healing from such traumatic events.

This research assumes a deeply empathetic stance, striving to provide a platform for these young survivors to articulate their exceptional experiences. By shedding light on their narratives, this study aspires to create enhanced understanding of the interplay between trauma and the cognitive processes that infuse their experiences with meaning, significance, and a path towards healing.

On July 8, 2014, roughly a fortnight following the commencement of Ramadan that year, the Israeli occupation government initiated a military campaign known as "Operation Protective Edge" within the Gaza Strip. This campaign unfolded against the backdrop of deeply rooted historical and geopolitical tensions, and it had significant psychological and emotional implications for the individuals and communities directly affected by the conflict. "We couldn't believe that Israel did that to us," Um Hani, a Palestinian woman, told me in our interview conducted two years after war. "We witnessed wars before and shelling against Hamas locations, but this war targeted the civilians. People were running everywhere, stepping on the dead bodies."

The Israeli assault on Palestinians in the Gaza Strip repeated instances of violence prior to the 2014 war. In both 2008 and 2012, Israel occupation initiated military operations within Gaza, notably "Operation Cast Lead" in 2008, which resulted in the tragic loss of over 1,400 Palestinian lives and left thousands wounded. [1] Heartbreakingly, among the casualties were 431 children, with an additional 1,606 suffering grievous injuries, including the loss of limbs, eyesight, and hearing. [2]

However, the 2014 war, also known as "Operation Strong Cliff," held a distinct and troubling characteristic. During this period, children constituted the majority of those affected by the conflict.[3] What sets this particular military campaign apart is the assertion that these children were not merely unintended victims caught up in the chaos of war; rather, they appeared to be the primary and deliberate targets of a military campaign aimed at the destruction of both these children and their communities. The

---

[1] B'Tselem, n.d.

[2] UAT Coalition, 2009.

[3] PCHR, 2014.

deliberate nature of such a comprehensive assault raises critical questions about the intentions behind these actions, as it suggests that Israeli forces were fully aware that their operations were directly focused on children, resulting in the tragic loss of life.

To demonstrate the pronounced effects on children, this book depicts a small portion of the attacks Palestinian children and their families have suffered, told by first-hand witnesses like Um Hani. She described to me the inescapability of the bombs, which came fast and without warning. There was no way to prepare for the attacks, nowhere to run and hide:

> We used to have a balcony, and the children used to play in the olive field. I told them to go away or they might be targeted as the aircrafts don't differentiate between children and adults. One of them, who came recently from Saudi Arabia, had just walked there [indicating with her hand a place nearby], and the aircraft targeted him. I saw them flying in the sky, and I was screaming. I wanted to get down to help him, but I couldn't as my daughters were screaming. I had no clue what to do; I was walking in the house screaming. My husband asked my children about me, and they told him I was in the house screaming.

The enduring conflict in the Gaza Strip has inflicted profound and lasting trauma upon its residents, spanning multiple generations. Over the years, various studies have illuminated the devastating impact of war-related trauma on the Palestinian population, rendering them a deeply traumatized nation.[4] Palestinian children have borne the brunt of this ongoing strife, grappling with the stress of warfare and its horrors. Recent studies have shed light on the continued suffering faced by these children, while psychologists analyze the cumulative effects of past violence, death, and the constant fear that permeates their daily lives.

The 2014 Israeli military operation not only left a trail of widespread infrastructure destruction but also resulted in a significant loss of life

---

[4] Altawil et al., 2008; Baker, 1990; Hein et al., 1993; Qouta & El Sarraj, 2002.

among Palestinians. Between 2,145 and 2,251 Palestinians lost their lives during this operation,[5] with a staggering 70% of the casualties identified as civilians, including approximately 257-299 women and 501-556 children.[6] Additionally, there were 379 individuals whose identities remain unknown.[7]

One of the most distressing aspects of this conflict was the fact that a single Israeli attack could claim the lives of multiple members of Palestinian families, leading to the loss of 739 family members from 142 Palestinian households. Beyond the immediate loss of life, the repercussions are far-reaching. As many as 6,000 children now grapple with the reality of having a parent who has sustained a lifelong disability, while 1,500 children have been orphaned as a result of Israeli attacks that claimed their parents' lives.[8] Furthermore, according to a United Nations report from October 9, 2014, the Palestinian Ministry of Health reported that a staggering 11,100 Palestinians were injured during this conflict, including 410 elderly individuals, 2,088 women, and 3,374 children. Tragically, this translates to 1,000 Palestinian children facing a lifetime of disability.

----

[5] Al Mezan Center for Human Rights, 2016; Palestinian Center for Human Rights, 2014; United Nations Office for the Coordination of Humanitarian Affairs [UN OCHA], 2015b; Zonszein, 2015.

[6] Casualty numbers varied by source. Based on U.N. OCHA sources, at least 2,205 Palestinians were killed during Operation Protective Edge by October 17, 2014. *The Guardian* reported that 2,145 Palestinians, including 1,492 civilians, were killed (Zonszein, 2015). The Al Mezan Center for Human Rights (2016), on the other hand, reported a total of 2,251 Palestinians were killed, while the Palestinian Center for Human Rights (PCHR, 2014) reported the total number of Palestinian fatalities at 2,216, of whom 1,543 were civilians (70% of the total number of victims). The civilian victims included 293 women and 556 children. Based on the U.N. Development Programme (2015) report, 501 children, 257 women, and 379 unidentified individuals were killed, and in total at least 1,473 civilians were killed. According to the PCHR (2014), 1,660 Palestinian civilians were killed, including 527 children and 299 women. Al Mezan (2016) reported that the vast majority of those killed were civilians, including 551 children and 299 women.

[7] PCHR (2014); Al Mezan Center for Human Rights, 2016.

[8] UN, 2014b.

The psychological toll on all children in Gaza is undeniable, as they grapple with the pervasive crisis. Indeed, the report highlights that no less than 373,000 children in the region require immediate and specialized psychosocial support to cope with the enduring trauma of their circumstances.[9] Symptoms of children's trauma included wetting the bed, clinging to parents, and nightmares. In UNICEF's July 28, 2014, report "No Safe Place for Children in Gaza," the head of UNICEF's Gaza office, Pernille Ironside, said, "The physical and psychological toll that the violence is having on people is almost indescribable ... We see children killed, injured, mutilated and burnt, in addition to being terrified to their core."[10] Moreover, the enduring hazard of unexploded bombs, remnants of Israeli military operations in the Gaza Strip, continues to imperil the lives of Palestinian civilians, particularly children. This grim reality disrupted the education of nearly half a million Palestinian children in the Gaza Strip, preventing them from commencing the school year on August 24, 2014, as armed conflict raged. According to the United Nations Development Programme's report titled "One Year After - Gaza Early Recovery and Reconstruction Needs Assessment," 217 schools and 60 kindergartens suffered damage, with 18 of these structures rendered irreparable.[11] The effects of the destruction of schools affects people of all ages, as many of these educational facilities were transformed into shelters for over 100,000 Palestinians who became homeless by Israeli attacks.[12]

In addition to the physical destruction, the daily lives of students were further burdened by severe challenges. Frequent power outages, lasting up to 18-20 hours a day, limited their access to computers and nighttime study. Prior to the 2014 Israeli offensive, Palestinian children in Gaza already grappled with severe educational limitations imposed by Israeli restrictions. Importing educational materials such as books proved exceedingly difficult, resulting in a dire shortage.

---

[9] UN, 2014b.

[10] Welbel, 2014, "No safe place," para. 3.

[11] UN Development Programme, 2015, p. 25.

[12] IMEU, 2014 Aug.

Moreover, the strict separation enforced by Israel between Gaza and the West Bank hindered Palestinian students' access to educational opportunities.[13] According to the Institute for Middle East Understanding, only three Gazan college students, recipients of U.S. government scholarships, were granted entry into the West Bank between 2000 and 2012. Meanwhile, universities in the occupied West Bank offered academic disciplines and degrees that were unavailable in Gaza. These systemic barriers destroyed the aspirations of Palestinian youth and their families for a better future.[14]

It is noteworthy that the 2014 Israeli occupation in Gaza inflicted more devastation and casualties than the two preceding major assaults, with a disproportionately high number of Gazan children losing their lives.[15] An investigation conducted by Defense for Children International Palestine in 2014 revealed that Palestinian children aged 6 and older in the Gaza Strip had endured three major Israeli military offensives, including Operation Cast Lead (2008-9) and Operation Pillar of Defense (2012).[16] Tragically, 8 out of every 10 of Gaza's 900,000 children were dependent on humanitarian assistance, according to the United Nations Development Program.[17] Additionally, the majority of Palestinian children aged 7 and below had spent their entire lives under the unlawful siege and blockade imposed by Israeli occupation since 2007.

Generations of Palestinian families and their children continue to cope with the long-term effects of war, holding space in their grief for both the survivors and the generations lost. One of Um Hani's sons, who was killed in the bombings in 2014, was precious to her, and a great loss. Before his death, the son and his wife had been undergoing an in-vitro fertilization process, so the son was resolute to remain at home when the shelling started.

---

[13] At one point, Israeli occupation blocked the importation of writing paper, notebooks, and pencils, leading to a shortage of the latter, too.

[14] IMEU, 2014 Feb.

[15] B'Tselem, n.d.; Stein, 2013.

[16] DCIP, 2014.

[17] U.N. Development Programme, 2015.

My son refused to leave and insisted to stay because he needed to work in order to pay the expenses of his wife's artificial insemination pregnancy. He made his living from his chicken farm.

The in-vitro process was halted due to the tragedy of the intended father's death.

Israel has also employed a comprehensive strategy of economic and physical constraints on the Gaza Strip, with an intensified focus since June 2007. [18] As documented by Human Rights Watch, these measures, including the closure of Gaza, severe restrictions on Palestinian mobility, and tight controls on the flow of goods, have had profound and ongoing repercussions on the entire Palestinian civilian populace, particularly impacting children. This multifaceted Israeli occupation approach includes family separations and limited access to essential healthcare, educational opportunities, and economic prospects, exacerbating unemployment and poverty levels.

The cumulative effect of these Israeli policies has compelled a staggering 70% of Gaza's population to depend on humanitarian aid for their basic needs.[19] The blockade encompasses measures that curtail Palestinians' access to fundamental necessities such as food, water, and electricity. Furthermore, it imposes strict prohibitions on Palestinians seeking to leave the Gaza Strip, even for vital medical treatments, while exerting tight control over all Gaza's borders.

Equally noteworthy is the deployment of psychological tactics aimed at inflicting mental and emotional distress upon the population. These methods involve the persistent presence of drones flying overhead day and night, the use of snipers targeting Palestinian individuals, and

---

[18] In June 2007, the Islamic Resistance Movement (Hamas) came to power (democratically elected in 2006), and in response the Israeli and U.S. governments led international economic and political boycotts on the Gaza Strip.

[19] Human Rights Watch, 2017.

periodic bombings, all contributing to an atmosphere of perpetual fear and instability.

> It was a tragedy that one of my sons was a martyr and the other was wounded. The wounded son is very nervous after the incident because he was accompanied by his brother who was martyred—(he) saw the death of his brother. One went to the hospital while the other to the graveyard. The wound remains inside me, that my son died before seeing his child.
>
> —Um Hani

The Impact of War & the Focus of this Study

Research has demonstrated that wars can inflict severe psychological distress, affecting individuals across all age groups, including young children and infants.[20] These distressing effects can stem from exposure to both natural disasters and human-made threats that jeopardize the victims' safety and that of their families.[21] While the psychological repercussions of natural disasters are well-documented, our focus here is exclusively on the enduring ramifications of war, particularly in the context of children in various nations, including the Palestinian territories.[22]

It is essential to acknowledge that war exerts catastrophic consequences on the well-being and health of individuals directly involved and those residing in proximity to conflict zones.[23] In fact, conflicts and wars are

---

[20] Abu-Saba, 1999; Barnett & Finnemore, 1999; Cairns & Dawes, 1996; Goldstein, Wampler, & Wise, 1997; Javidi & Yadollahie, 2012; Joseph, Williams, & Yule, 1997; Saltzman, Layne, Steinberg, Arslanagic, & Pynoos, 2003; Thulesius & Hakansson, 1999; Vander Kolk, McFarlane, & Weisaeth, 1996; Weine et al., 1995.

[21] Ahmad et al., 2000; Ajdukovic, 1998; Altawil et al., 2008; Arroyo & Eth, 1985; Baker, 1990; Baker & Shalhoub-Kevorkian, 1999; Eth, 2008; Garbarino, Kostelny, & Dubrow, 1991b.

[22] Nader, Pynoos, Fairbanks, Al-Ajeel, & Al-Asfour, 1993.

[23] Summerfield, 1997.

known to cause greater mortality and disability than most major diseases and even natural disasters.[24] My personal background as an individual born and raised in the war-torn region of Palestine has deeply influenced the direction of this research. I have drawn upon my own experiences to gain insight into the profound trauma and suffering endured by survivors of armed conflicts.

The subjectivity that I, as a researcher, bring to this work has played a pivotal role in creating an environment where participants feel safe and understood, thereby enabling them to openly share their experiences of suffering. As someone personally affected by war, I firmly believe that war cannot be encapsulated solely in academic discourse. Instead, the narrative form is imperative in unveiling the experiential truth that war constitutes a living nightmare, both during the conflict and in its aftermath. My primary objective is to amplify the voices of survivors, including my own, who yearn daily for an end to the horrors of war.

It is crucial to emphasize that the profound impact of war on the human psyche eludes the comprehension of those who have not personally experienced life in a war zone. A purely academic work falls short in conveying the authentic human dimension of war, which not only robs individuals of their humanity but also leaves them bearing the enduring scars—physical, emotional, and psychological.

War is a complex and multifaceted phenomenon, often defined as a state of armed conflict between different nations, states, or groups, characterized by the use of force, violence, and organized military actions to achieve political, territorial, or ideological objectives. One widely cited definition of war comes from Carl von Clausewitz, a renowned Prussian military theorist: "War is the continuation of politics by other means." This perspective underscores the inherent link between war and political goals—how nations and groups resort to armed conflict to advance their strategic interests and resolve disputes. This definition illustrates the profound impact of war on societies, economies, and international relations, making it a subject of deep concern and study for scholars, policymakers, and

---

[24] Murthy & Lakshminarayana, 2006, "Abstract," para. 6.

global citizens alike. While this definition provides valuable insights into the nature of war, it is essential to acknowledge that the concept of war has evolved over time, and contemporary conflicts often involve non-state actors and unconventional forms of warfare, challenging traditional definitions.[25]

In the context of this book, the term "war" is employed to designate conflicts characterized by military actions targeting civilian populations, even when such conflicts lack formal declarations of war. The focus of our investigation is exclusively centered on the aftermath of the Israeli military operations on Palestinian children residing in the Gaza Strip. Our purpose is to examine the subsequent psychological challenges, emphasizing the imperative need for targeted interventions, therapeutic measures, and long-term strategizing to assist traumatized children in coping with the aftermath of their experiences. As stated by Murthy & Lakshminarayana:

> War destroys communities and families and often disrupts the development of the social and economic fabric of nations. The effects of war include long-term physical and psychological harm to children and adults, as well as reduction in material and human capital. Death as a result of wars is simply the "tip of the iceberg."

In addition to death, other consequences include "endemic poverty, malnutrition, disability, economic/social decline and psychosocial illness."[26] War trauma leaves permanent physical and psychological marks on humans.[27] In some parts of the world, including Palestine, generation after generation has grown up knowing only war. The World Health Organization has asserted that, during military violence, an estimated

---

[25] Clausewitz, 1989.

[26] Murthy & Lakshminarayana, 2006, "Abstract," para. 6.

[27] Summerfield, 1997.

10% of the people who experience traumatic events will have serious mental health problems and another 10% will develop behavior that will hinder their ability to function effectively.[28] The most common conditions are depression, anxiety, and psychosomatic problems such as insomnia, or back and stomach aches.[29]

The psychological trauma created by war is one of the most prominent illnesses that children of war suffer. Psychological trauma is indeed one of the most significant and devastating consequences for children who are exposed to wars and armed conflicts. This trauma can have long-lasting and profound effects on their mental and emotional well-being. Some of the most prominent illnesses that children of war suffer is psychological trauma, PTSD, depression and anxiety, loss and grief, disruption in education, physical health issues, social isolation, desensitization to violence, and interference with psychological development.

Throughout various regions worldwide, the psychological ramifications of armed conflicts on children have been extensively documented. These regions include South Africa, Afghanistan, Cambodia, Kuwait, Bosnia and Herzegovina, as well as locations within Palestine, the Balkans, Iraq, and Lebanon.[30] Notably, studies indicate that the impact of war-related trauma on children's mental health can be enduring and severe.

For instance, in the aftermath of the Cambodian conflict, a significant number of children (50%) exhibited symptoms of post traumatic stress disorder (PTSD) and depression four years after the cessation of hostilities.[31] A follow-up assessment conducted fifteen years

---

[28] WHO, 2001.

[29] Murthy & Lakshminarayana, 2006, "Abstract," para. 7.

[30] Realmuto et al., 1992; Sack, Clarke, & Seeley, 1995; Mghir, Freed, Raskin, & Katon, 1995; Dawes, 1990; Smith, Perrin, Yule, & Rabe-Hesketh, 2001; Ajdukovic, 1998; Zivcic, 1993; Nader et al., 1993; El-Khosondar, 2004; Hawajri, 2003; Qouta & El-Sarraj, 2004; Sen & Sibai, 2000; Ahmad et al., 2000.

[31] Kinzie, Sack, Angell, Manson, & Rath, 1986.

later revealed that a substantial proportion of Cambodian young adults (24%) still grappled with PTSD, with 59% experiencing PTSD at some point in their lives.[32]

During the Yugoslavian wars, a substantial portion (25%) of Bosnian adolescents who had resettled in the United States displayed symptoms of PTSD, while 17% suffered from depression.[33] Furthermore, a striking 70% of Kuwaiti children experienced varying degrees of PTSD following the Gulf War,[34] with similar rates found among Kurdish children who had been displaced.[35]

The emotional toll of war was also evident in Croatia, where depressive symptoms affected all children during the conflict. However, research revealed that displaced (refugee) children exhibited higher levels of sadness and fear when compared to their local counterparts who had not been uprooted from their homes.[36]

In addition to the commonly observed PTSD symptoms in war-affected children, it is imperative to acknowledge that trauma engenders a range of mental health challenges for these young victims. It is also important to note that the definition and understanding of psychological trauma may vary across different cultural contexts. According to the National Institute of Mental Health, psychological trauma is defined as

> an emotionally painful, shocking, stressful, and sometimes life-threatening experience. It may or may not involve physical injuries and can result from witnessing distressing events. Examples include a natural disaster, physical or sexual abuse, and terrorism. Disasters such as hurricanes, earthquakes, and floods can claim lives, destroy homes or whole communities,

---

[32] Hubbard, Realmuto, Northwood, and Masten, 1995.

[33] Weine et al., 1995.

[34] Nader, Pynoos, Fairbanks, Al-Ajeel, and Al-Asfour, 1993.

[35] Ahmad, 1992.

[36] Zivcic, 1993.

and cause serious physical and psychological injuries. Trauma can also be caused by acts of violence.[37]

Research that explores cultural variations should investigate how perceived trauma affects children across different cultures in order to accurately assess its impact. One important concept to consider is "cultural bereavement," which refers to the experience of individuals who migrate, either by force or by choice, and the losses they encounter.[38] This includes the loss of social and cultural support systems, as well as aspects of their own identity. To illustrate, when studying a child refugee's experience of trauma, researchers should examine how the child perceives the trauma, how they communicate distress through rituals, and the cultural strategies they employ to overcome it.

However, it's worth noting that certain coping mechanisms and protective factors may transcend cultural and societal differences. In a review of the psychological effects of war on children, Jensen and Shaw emphasized that children possess cognitive immaturity, adaptability, and innate resilience, which can serve as safeguards against trauma in relatively less severe wartime conditions.[39]

Nevertheless, whether direct exposure to war has an immediate negative impact on mental health or not, prolonged exposure to terrorism and war can undermine civil society, endangering children. This phenomenon has been observed in places like Mozambique, Belfast, and various refugee camps in the late 20th century. In cases of massive trauma, a child's entire ecological system collapses, whether due to natural disasters or war.[40] When their familiar order disintegrates into chaos, children may resort to associating with terrorists, forming gangs, or engaging in violent behavior if they perceive these actions as a means of protection.

---

[37] National Institute of Mental Health, "What is trauma?" para. 2, 2015.

[38] Eisenbruch, 1991.

[39] Jensen and Shaw 1993 in Thabet & Vostanis, 1999, p. 389.

[40] Wright et al., 1997.

The collapse of civil society, often resulting from bombings and large-scale attacks, can pose a long-term psychological threat to children greater than the trauma of war itself.

It's important to recognize that the impact of war extends to Israeli children as well, but this research specifically focuses on Palestinian children due to their unique circumstances as a refugee population within Palestine. Consequently, this study employs distinct metrics to comprehend and address the Palestinian dilemma. The primary emphasis of this research is on the human experience and the emotional-psychological repercussions faced by Palestinian children during the war, intentionally avoiding a political examination. This research underscores the significance of distinguishing between mental health issues arising from the Gaza war of 2014 and the political aspects and agendas associated with it. As a Palestinian academic researcher, my intention was to redefine the mental health paradigm resulting from the 2014 Gaza Strip conflict, with a primary focus on the human experience, quality of life, and human rights.

Too often, the physical and psychological toll of war on children's lives is either inadequately addressed or overlooked.[41] Alongside various non-trauma-specific psychological issues, post-traumatic stress disorder (PTSD) has become a prevalent psychiatric diagnosis for those exposed to warlike conditions.[42] Childhood trauma can also leave enduring marks on cognitive development, moral and personality growth, interpersonal relationships, and coping abilities.[43]

According to reports from the United Nations Children's Fund (UNICEF), it is evident that the consequences of war inflict long-term harm on children, encompassing physical and psychological aspects. While child mortality is an undeniable tragedy of war, it merely scratches the surface of the profound hardships that children endure during conflict.[44] These consequences, often under-documented, include persistent poverty,

---

[41] Machel, 2001.

[42] Summerfield, 1997.

[43] Arroyo & Eth, 1985.

[44] Cf. UNICEF, 2005.

malnutrition, disability, socioeconomic decline, psychosocial ailments, and more. This study reveals that the traumatic effects of war and its aftermath on Palestinian children are enduring, leading to long-term issues such as mental health disorders and behavioral challenges that persist throughout their lives.

The evolving reality suggests that the Palestinian nation is grappling with a profound collective trauma.[45] Over time, the afflictions resulting from war trauma have contributed to a dysfunctional society. However, if left untreated, fear and trauma can become normalized and accepted as routine aspects of life.[46] To address this, it is crucial to recognize that mental suffering extends beyond narrow medical indicators related to physical injury and illness. This research strives to draw attention to the pressing need for greater focus on the mental health and emotional scars experienced by children in the Gaza Strip due to the war. There should be a corresponding shift in humanitarian aid to address the overwhelming mental health needs of these affected children. Through sharing their stories and experiences, my goal is to raise significant awareness that will mobilize a robust response from mental health professionals and the international community.

---

[45] Ahmad, Sofi, Sundelin-Wahlsten, & Von Knorring, 2000; Altawil, Nel, Asker, Samara, & Harrold, 2008; Arroyo & Eth, 1985; Dawes, 1990; Eisenbruch, 1991; Wright, Masten, Northwood, & Hubbard, 1997.

[46] Baker & Shalhoub-Kevorkian, 1999; Eth, 2008; Farhood et al., 1993; Mousa & Madi, 2003; Summerfield, 1997.

CHAPTER 1:

"We are besieged, in prison and occupied"

Operation Protective Edge presented a stark example of war's effect on children and families in the Gaza Strip, due in large part to the battleground locations. Rather than opposing armies meeting on a remote battlefield, the battleground was located in the neighborhoods of the Palestinian people. Casualties were not limited to a few unlucky Palestinians who were accidentally caught in the crossfire. Entire homes and families were purposely wiped out with direct missile and bomb hits, so most survivors lost more than one close relative. Thus, the participants' experiences are overwhelming, catastrophic, and barely survivable, and explain the widespread grief, despair, and trauma that these people continue to experience.

The 2014 war placed all of Palestine's children living in these areas in the target sights of the Israeli army and led to large amounts of trauma in the surviving child victims. A total of 551–578 Palestinian children (depending on reporting source) were killed during the July/August 2014 conflict, and another 3,374 children were injured.[47] The direct experience of children suffering from the impact of Operation Protective Edge (also called Strong Cliff) is expressed most clearly through the personal accounts of parents and children.[48] Rought-Brooks chronicles the experiences of the parents of these children firsthand:

> I saw a man who had lost his daughter while running—he wanted to carry her but they told him not to and he lost her.

---

[47] UN, 2014b.

[48] Rought-Brooks, 2015.

I saw a tiny one-week-old baby left in the street and I picked him up. We took him with us and announced that we had found this baby and for someone to come and pick him up.[49]

The most disturbing reports involved eye-witness accounts of the deaths of children. One mother, in tears, relates the devastating loss of three of her children during the war:

One of my sons, Ibrahim, went outside and there was a drone missile and he was killed. A man came to tell me—Ibrahim was killed. They wanted to take Ibrahim to the hospital and my oldest son went on a motorbike with my brother-in-law to the hospital—but they were also hit and they were killed. Ten days later they bombed our house over our heads and my 13-year-old daughter was killed in the bombing.[50]

In my research for this book, I also interviewed mental health workers who provide an intimate, hands-on perspective of the resulting scourge of mental health issues that plague Gaza as a result of the continual violence and war. Dr. Kamal Qadih, Ph.D. in Psychology, from Algeria, works as a psychologist at Al-Ghad Al-Mashreq Association in the Khuza'a area of Khan Yunis. He described the attacks by Israeli forces:

As a result of the war in 2014, there was very significant psychological damage and consequences because of the intense aggressiveness and devastating impact of the attacks, which increased from previous wars, leaving people unprepared.

Most people, especially children, were trapped in the Khuza'a area, and were attacked by tanks and aircraft with direct fire and direct rocket fire from the aircraft. The injuries that resulted

---

[49] Rought-Brooks, 2015, p. 20.

[50] Ibid.

from this war were very devastating. Some people's stomachs were amputated as a direct result of Israeli aircraft missiles and the fire from Israeli tanks.

Some of the surviving people of Gaza related to me their firsthand experiences of the death, destruction, and injuries they suffered, and detailed their accounts with moment-to-moment recollections of their harrowing near-death experiences.

Wahdan is a man in his 50s who identified himself as a teacher from Beit Hanoun. He has three boys (Musab, Omar, and Mohammed). When I interviewed Wahdan, he and all three of his sons were still recovering from the last Israeli offensive in 2014, in which they were all severely injured. Wahdan sat in a small spot in what he calls home now, confined to his electric wheelchair. He shared his story of how his home was bombed:

> I am a resident of Beit Hanoun. During the war, the shelling was fierce in Beit Hanoun, and we had to flee the area to the camp. We rented a house in the camp in the Caliph area and we stayed in it.
>
> In two to three days, we were bombed. The Israelis bombed us with three or four bombshells using war aircraft and drones. We were trapped at home and bombing increased, and the houses around us were destroyed.

Wahdan told a tale we would hear again and again, of children and families forced to flee for their lives in the middle of the night, with tragic results. "The situation was extremely difficult," he continued. "My wife was killed, my legs were amputated, I have shell fragments in my stomach, and my three children were seriously injured." When the Israelis bombed their home, Wahdan lost 12 family members total, including his wife (the mother of Musab, Omar, and Mohammed) and parents. The three boys were injured in the head and stomach.

Um Fadi is a Palestinian woman who took precautions against the bombing, but to no avail. She relates what happened to her children:

My daughter and I were preparing a meal to break the fast. We then decided to do the dishes while the food cooked. As we walked towards the dishwashing sink, I was carrying the dishwashing sponge, and my daughter the dishwashing towel, when suddenly, a missile hit the ground next to us.

My house had lots of glass windows and is close to the street, causing any bombing to have great impact. When the missile hit my house, I jumped - I have no idea how high. My daughter grabbed me by the staircase.

I was partly unconscious. I was asking, Where are we going? Where are we going? I was telling them we need to flee the house, but they would not listen.

As with many others attempting to survive, but with nowhere to go, Um Fadi and her family remained in their home until it was impossible to stay.

On the second day, we were sleeping in the bedroom. Usually, when the fighting intensifies, we all sleep in the same room out of our fear. At 2 a.m. I heard the sound of a barrel bomb hitting the Alsidiqeen (the Righteous) Mosque. When they bombed the Mosque, I was covered in glass. We were sleeping. My son was sleeping by the window because the weather was so hot.

Suddenly, the window was shattered to pieces and fell into the middle of the room. The room where we slept, the bathroom windows, and the door, were all broken down. There was no light because the electricity was cut off, and my daughter was screaming.

I was so confused and disoriented that I hugged a gallon of water thinking that it was my 2-year-old son. I could not differentiate night from day. My husband took the kids and me, and we fled to the school.

For those who survived, the most horrific results of the bombings occurred right in front of their eyes, and the shock from what they saw remains embedded in their minds. Um Fadi told me:

> I saw one of our relatives killed. He was walking with his mother. I couldn't bear the scene. His mother could not come back with his brother to help her son. The bombing was from every side. They could not save him. If they would have been allowed to help him, he might be alive now.

Asmaa, a Palestinian mother, still suffers seriously from physical, emotional, and mental injuries after being bombed. She lost her children and family members who were sitting right next to her when the bombs struck, and she is one of many afflicted with a variety of ills that have changed her entire life. She told me the harrowing tale of fear and sorrow and spoke for her daughter, who had been severely traumatized. She recounts,

> I fled my home under very devastating circumstances. The Israeli shelling reached the footsteps of my door. I was seven months pregnant. It was very difficult to flee the Beit Hanoun area. I mean, the Israelis were about to reach my home door. I called one of our relatives. I asked him if he could help me flee the area. He agreed but he requested that I pay him. I told him I will pay you whatever you want but just help my children and me flee the Beit Hanoun area.

Asmaa lost 12 family members, was forced to flee the bombing and go to the Red Crescent, then to a house in Jabalia, then to her sister's house. Her sister's home was bombed and her sister was killed with her husband, and Asmaa was seriously injured. Her nephew, daughter, husband, and son were also injured:

We were in our home in Beit Hanoun, but the Israelis started shelling us. Then we fled Beit Hanoun to Jabalia camp. We stayed in Jabalia camp for a while, then my uncle came and took me and the kids to Beit Lahia to stay with him.

We stayed in a house near the Caliphs Mosque and there we were bombarded by the Israelis. The occupation shelled two rockets by the drones into the heart of the house we were staying in.

Asmaa's story reflects that of many Palestinian mothers who tried to save their children during the bombings, but just did not have enough arms to hold all of them, or enough strength to carry them and run.

My daughter was sleeping beside me, both our eyes were injured. I woke up, everything was dark, the ruins on top of us and there is smoke. The room was full of my children, and my little girl was sleeping beside me.

When I woke up after the Israeli bombardment, I was injured everywhere in my body. I looked around, I saw my daughter, I carried her and started running. I didn't see what happened to my other children in the room. I just took the little one and tried to get her out.

I was seven months pregnant, and I found my girl bleeding from the face and the chest. People took me and my daughter to the hospital.

Um Hani, who was quoted in the Introduction, spoke on behalf of her deceased son and her other traumatized children during our interview. "During the war of 2014 you definitely went through a difficult situation," I said. "All the houses were destroyed! Can you describe this painful incident which you went through?"

Six houses were destroyed—four here and two houses in Al-Ezba, northern Gaza, near Beit Hanoun, my sons' houses. The Israeli soldiers told us to evacuate the Juhor ad-Dik area, southern Gaza.

However, we did not heed the warning. The children and my daughters-in-law fled into another area where I rented a house for them in Zawaydah.

Um Salah faced similar problems to other Palestinian mothers, as her children, Moayad, Ghada, and Hammoda, were seriously injured and still suffer physically and psychologically from what happened:

They told us to get out of our homes and I refused to go out and stayed in my house. All those around me came out except me. My sister was with me in the house.

Suddenly I felt a strong concussion and looked around me. The house was destroyed; they had hit it with a missile. My son was about to enter the house and all of his body was buried except his face, and the girl and the boy were in the room.

My husband came to take the boy and the girl. I was injured in my feet and thank the Lord my injury is light, not like them.

My son's name is Moayad. He has internal bleeding in his stomach. They put him in the operating room for an urgent operation and my daughter was also injured in her stomach and also bleeding. Hammoda was injured in his face, light shrapnel, here was a fragment (indicated by her hand) but they removed it all.

Along with Um Salah, I spoke with one of her children. "Ghada, can you tell us how you got injured?" I asked. The child pointed to her hand. "Stones fell on me. While I was sleeping next to Hammoda, my mother and my aunt were looking at the window. Then a missile hit me in my stomach."

Wa'd, a girl of 16, along with her family, has also seen too much: When we fled from the house it was 12:30 am. We fled while the Israelis were bombing. My mother was slow to walk, my father was carrying my little brother who was shivering. As we were walking, the shelling intensified, the houses were falling down and the ruins were falling on us. A shell shrapnel was about to enter my mother's belly. The situation was very ugly and terrifying. I was thinking to myself, my mother could die in front of our eyes and we cannot help her.

Another child, Yazan, told me that he and his family were home when they were bombed before escaping to the Alhawuz area. He recalled drones and tanks attacking. "The drones and the tanks shelled me and I was injured. They shot me in the stomach," he said, pointing with his hand to the place of injury. "My dad took me to Dr. Kamal's clinic for treatment."

Among the many wounded, some wished to remain unidentified during our interviews. One such person, an immigrant with a now disabled son, spoke to me about their experience fleeing the bombing:

> Our house was shelled and we had to get out in the street. So, people are all running to the shelters. We ran with the people on the street until we got to my uncle's house in the center of the city. When we arrived at my uncle's house, we thought it was safer but it was not, it was bombed. They were fleeing the bombing, and because of fear, they forgot to take me with them.
>
> This is my disabled son. His legs were folded and it was very difficult for us to move and to escape from one place to another. Seeing people in the street running away in large numbers was like the scene of migration.

In another interview, an anonymous father introduced his son, Muhammad, and recounted what happened to them:

> When they bombed the house in the war of 2014, shrapnel struck his head and opened it from here [pointing]; his skull was broken and his scalp got torn.

Also, it caused him deep psychological scars. This is where the injuries occurred [pointing with his hand to Muhammad's head]. It was a huge injury, but the Lord saved and protected him.

Now he is receiving psychological therapy, but the trauma was so severe that his condition is getting worse day by day. Such are the effects of the war. I asked Muhammad to recount his experience of these events. He recalls,

> They bombarded us during the war, and we tried to escape. They took me to the hospital, and I stayed for six days to receive treatment. Then when we came back home, the Israelis shelled our house, and my dad had to take me to the hospital for treatment once again.

When asked where he was injured, Muhammad pointed to his head:

> When they started shelling us, we escaped to the Alhawuz area and stayed with others in their home. They had bombed our house while we were still inside it. Even when we ran away, they continued to shell us. My head was injured and split open. We managed to escape to the hospital, where I received medical treatment.

Raghad and Maysaa are sisters who escaped the bombing together with their family, but not without severe consequences:

> My mother and I stayed in our room. My mom was looking for me and she was asking, 'Where is Raghad?' Suddenly a rocket came towards me, the missile exploded and suffocated all of us with gas. We could not escape.

> Later, we managed to escape through the window and went to Ismaeel's house. We sat outside. Then a missile hit my brother and he died suddenly. Shrapnel from the missile hit my hand.

I asked her where on her hand she was injured, and she pointed to it.

Then we went back to Mahmood's house. Then we fled, but the Israelis were watching us. Then they took me to a European hospital.

Raghad still had the piece of shrapnel that was extracted from her hand in the hospital, and opened a container to show me.

Raghad's sister, Maysaa, continued, telling a harrowing tale of a family fleeing for their lives and the unfortunate fate that each one of them met:

We were sitting at home when the windows got knocked out. We closed the door and sat for about 5 minutes. We felt terrified because the situation was extremely difficult. We sat and our oldest brother told us that the room near the street was not safe. He advised us to stand and to protect our heads.

As I was entering the room with my oldest brother, they bombed the house. The house was in flames, and we started screaming. My dad was sitting here [in the living room]. My brother Mahmood kept calling to my dad while we were screaming from fear. Then Mahmood told us, may God help you, keep the door closed, I have to go and find Dad. He got my dad and brought him inside the room covered with blood. We got so scared and started to scream.

The smoke [white phosphorous smoke] was coming into the room from under the door. The room had become so filled with smoke that we couldn't see each other. We opened the window so that we could breathe, but the smoke smothered us inside and out. My brothers and I sat against the wall, from which I extended my legs out.

My oldest brother couldn't see us in this situation, so he broke the window and started screaming at other people to take us out. He screamed, Ameen and Huthiyfa, take my siblings! My siblings are dying! Help me to take them out! They told him to wait, then finally placed a chair under the window, and started helping us to get out one by one.

At this point, we got to one of our neighbor's homes. They started to wash us with water and told us that we need to stay inside. Then they brought us some milk to drink. We were very tired. As we were sitting inside feeling safe, suddenly a missile hit the house. The missile was so powerful that we all ran outside. My sister Raghad was injured, and I didn't know that my brother was killed at that point.

When we came out of the house, our neighbor, Ismaeel was saying Mahmood Ibn Tayseer was killed and his brother Jihad was killed, as well. My mom started screaming when she heard that my brother had been killed. We said may God have mercy upon him. I told my dad the news and I asked him to pray for my brother.

We escaped to yet another house. My mother became very tired. I took my sister with me and I found out that she had been injured. My oldest sister had been carrying her and tied her injured hand. We remained trapped until the next day when the Red Cross came to the Alhawuz area. Then the neighbors were telling us that whoever can come to the Alhawuz area needed to come now, and whoever is not capable of coming needs to stay.

My older sister took my younger sister Raghad and my other siblings with my dad and went to the Alhawuz area. My mother and I stayed at Mohammed Hamad's house. I was about to leave but my mom grabbed me by the hand because she thought my heart was overly tired, so she kept me with her. We stayed in the Alhawuz area.

After a while, we told them to go and send us an ambulance or the Red Cross. However, they returned and said that they were shooting at us. I immediately felt that I am not doing well and I felt numb. I took a chair to the stairs and sat there. Then the house was bombed and hundreds of bricks fell on us by the stairs. Nonetheless, we stayed inside. We then heard the voices of people who had come back from Alhawuz calling to us. The severely injured stayed but we got out. My mom held my hand as we walked through the unpaved way.

We reached the end of the street and my mother stopped. She couldn't walk anymore. I stopped with her. I couldn't walk on and leave my mom alone. My mom started looking towards our house. The tank was by the mosque and the people were screaming at her, [Run! Run!].

She could not walk. Suddenly, we saw a donkey wagon, so we rode it. People helped to push it. We were on the road under the blistering sun, so I became very exhausted. The combination of the gas and the pounding sun caused me to become numb and nauseous.

Then the Israelis ordered us to sit down, raise our hands, and give them our ID card. Due to our injury and sickness, we couldn't come down from the donkey wagon, so I stayed put with my mom. I raised my head towards the cactus trees, when I suddenly saw a tank coming towards us. Then, the people were screaming at each other, and they were saying, "Let's run from this area!" People replied, "You cannot run, because the drones will bomb you with missiles!"

Then we arrived at the sycamore fig tree. We found the Israelis standing there on the tank and they laughed. When I looked at them my mom turned my face away so I would not upset them.

The Israelis kept pushing us to the Al-Shuafin area. As we got closer, my uncles and my grandfather met me and my mother and they hugged us, kissing and crying. Then, they took my mother and me. Then my mother and I sat by the road with my uncles and grandfather because there were no cars or ambulances to take us somewhere for care.

Later, a car drove by and tried to take us to the Al-Askari hospital. While we were in the car, an ambulance stopped by and told the driver to take us to Al-Askari hospital, because they could see that we were hurt. My mother, siblings, and I arrived at the hospital.

At the Al-Askari hospital they refused to admit my mom, because her injuries were not severe enough. Hearing that, my mom fell to the ground unconscious, and my grandfather started to scream. The doctor came and said, "Bring her." We went upstairs and waited. My mother sat on the bed and I on an adjacent chair. My grandfather stayed with us. We drank water and juice and waited.

My mother went into a coma. We thought she had died. The doctors were screaming at each other and asked my brothers and my grandfather to leave the room. I stayed with her. The doctors came into the room, about 15 of them. They brought a heart revival machine to revive her. Then they decided that they had to transfer her to the intensive care at Nasser Hospital. After they transferred my mom to Nasser Hospital, I stayed in the room at Al-Askari hospital sitting on the bed. They came and gave me an IV to sustain me. I thought I was well.

One of the doctors from Nasser hospital called me at Al-Askari hospital to let me speak with my mother. My mother asked me to come to Nasser hospital to be with her. The hospital transferred me to Nasser Hospital. I got there during the night. They put me on IV as I prepared to receive treatment.

After a few days, my chest began to swell. The doctors concluded they could not help me much. Then, they told us that they are sending my mother outside of Gaza for treatment. I started to cry. I was telling myself it's not enough that my brother was killed, now my mom is leaving us. I became increasingly worried about my little sister and my other siblings. At least my father and brothers came to the hospital to be with me at this point.

Five minutes after the afternoon prayer, the doctors decided that I should be transferred to a hospital outside of Gaza. When they told me, I refused. I said, I want to stay here with my siblings. But I had no choice but to go. My grandfather traveled with me to the El Arish area of Egypt. I underwent surgery there, before they transferred me to a hospital in Ismailia, where I stayed for 25 days after they did three surgeries for me.

At El Arish my mom and I ended up in the same hospital, in the same intensive care unit. I was in the first bed and she was in the fourth one. Between her and I was a little girl on one bed and a man on another who was covered in blood and dust. I started to stare at him but they closed the curtain between us. After they took him out of the room, they opened the curtain again. The doctor told me that my mother's condition was critical. Then I started to think that my mom is not going to live.

The next day they transferred us to Ismailia Hospital by plane. I was admitted to the intensive care unit. When I awoke my grandfather was with me. My uncle who lives in Saudi Arabia called him. He told my grandfather that his daughter Iman had died. When my grandfather told me, I sank and I started to cry. I felt devastated. I started saying to myself—so all the girls have their mother for them in the hospital, but I have no one. I started to say to myself—O God, I wish my mother was with me. I wish my mother were okay and that I could talk to her on the phone right now.

From our interviews, I had known that the sisters' mother eventually passed away. I asked Maysaa to tell me more about how she felt when she found out that had happened. "I felt devastated and I wanted to cry, but I couldn't," she said.

"My grandfather came and I begged him to tell me the truth about whether my mom had died or not. He replied, 'No, you think that your mom has died.' I thought he was telling me the truth. Every day I would ask him for my mom and he would reply she is fine, that she was with my siblings."

I prompted, "I know that your grandfather tried not to tell you the news about your mother's death, but when you knew for certain that she had died, how did you feel?" Maysaa continued:

When I got back home, the first thing I noticed was that the whole area was upside down. The ambulance could not use any of the roads. So, I got off at the Rawdeen area, and walked with my grandfather.

My little sister and my nephews saw me while they were playing. My sister started calling me, "Maysaa, Maysaa, my sister Maysaa is back." My aunts and my older sister heard her. My oldest sister was saying to my aunts how I was going to explain to her what happened, to explain how my mother was killed.

I got to the front of the house and held my little sister between my arms. Everyone told me to put her down because I was not feeling well. I put her down and then greeted my oldest sister and my aunties.

As we sat together, I asked, "Where is my mother? I thought she was back."

They replied, "Yes, she is back." I then replied, "Where is she?" They told me, "She is in the hospital for care."

I then told my sister, "Okay, get up, take me there now." She replied, "In a bit, after you rest."

My little sister then told me that our mom is no longer living, that everyone was lying to me. The minute she told me that I broke down and started crying. Then my father came and started crying, and my little sister, who was sitting on my lap, started crying as well.

As part of the vast destruction from the Operation Protective Edge war on Gaza 2014, as described by the personal accounts above, Israel's excessive illegal use of weapons against Palestinian children led to the injuring, paralyzing, and killing of those children. The United Nations reported that at least 142 Palestinian families with three or more members were killed in a single Israeli attack, with a total of 739 deaths. As many as 1,500 children were orphaned after Israeli attacks killed their parents. It is estimated that 6,000 children will have a parent with a lifelong disability.[51] The DCIP reported some of these victims' stories:

---

[51] UN, 2014a.

Seven children from three families died together Sunday evening, July 20, in the Remal neighborhood of Gaza City. Two Israeli missiles killed Mohammad Hani Mohammad Hallaq, 2, his cousins Saji Hasan Akram Hallaq, 4, and Kenan, 6, alongside their neighbors Ibrahim Khalil Abed Ammar, 13, and his siblings ages 6 and 3. A third Israeli drone missile killed their neighbor Rahaf Akram Ismail Abu Juma'a.

On Monday afternoon, in the Sabra neighborhood of Gaza City, an Israeli aircraft targeted the al-Qassas home, killing nine family members, including six children. Isra' Yasser Khader al-Qassas, 12, and his siblings Yasmin, 8, Arwa, 6, and Samar, 3, were playing with their cousins, Lamia, 14, and Nesma, 10, when they died.

The al-Kilani family fled their home in the northern Gaza city of Beit Lahia to the Shuja'iyya neighborhood in Gaza City at the start of Israel's aerial assault. Following intense Israeli attacks on Shuja'iyya, the family relocated to the Salam apartment complex in the center of Gaza City.

On Monday evening, an F16 airstrike targeted their building, killing Reem Ibrahim Theeb al-Kilani, 12, and her four siblings, Sawsan, 11, Yasin, 9, Yasser, 8, and Elias, 4. Mahmoud Shaaban Mohammad Derbas, 16, was killed in the same strike.

A family in the Mahatta area of Deir al-Balah in central Gaza lost two cousins, Othman Salem Abdul-Majid Brai'em, 17, and Fadi Azmi Abdul-Majid Brai'em, 17, who was killed by a targeted drone missile while bringing their donkey water on their farmland.52Dina Rushdi Omar Hamada, 16, died when her house in Gaza City was targeted by a drone missile.

In the southern Gaza town of Rafah, 16-year-old Anas Mahmoud Hussein Muammar was targeted by a drone missile as he sat with his brothers on the balcony of their apartment, drinking coffee. He was pronounced dead in hospital after sustaining critical injuries.

---

52 "Ramallah, July 24, 2014," DCIP, 2014, paras. 3-7.

At Al-Bureij refugee camp in central Gaza, 12-year-old Shaaban Jamil Shaaban Zeyadeh was killed along with six of his family members as they tried to evacuate their home, which was bombed in an airstrike.

The names of the children from the Abu Jami' family in Khan Yunis, ages ranging from 4 months to 14 years old, are listed below. All were sheltering in their four-story house when the strike occurred without warning:

Njoud Tayseer Ahmad Abu Jami', 4 months

Bisan Bassam Ahmad Abu Jami', 6 months

Nour Yaser Ahmad Abu Jami', 2

Rinas Tayseer Ahmad Abu Jami', 2

Suheila Bassam Ahmad Abu Jami', 3

Seraj Yaser Ahmad Abu Jami', 4

Batoul Bassam Ahmad Abu Jami', 4

Tawfiq Ahmad Abu Jami', 4

Rayan Tayseer Ahmad Abu Jami', 5

Sajed Yaser Ahmad Abu Jami', 7

Maisa'a Tawfiq Ahmad Abu Jami', 7

Husam Abu Qnais, 7

Ahmad Tawfiq Ahmad Abu Jami', 8

Haifa Tawfiq Ahmad Abu Jami', 9

Ayyoub Tayseer Ahmad Abu Jami', 10

Aya Tawfiq Ahmad Abu Jami', 12

Fatima Tayseer Ahmad Abu Jami', 12

Jawdat Tawfiq Ahmad Abu Jami', 13

Razan Tawfiq Ahmad Abu Jami', 14.[53]

---

[53] "July 22 Update," DCIP, 2014, paras. 3-7.

Palestinian children have been affected by the imposition of arbitrary measures by Israeli occupation authorities. This alarming situation persists in defiance of numerous international agreements, treaties, covenants, and laws designed to safeguard the rights of children. Of paramount significance in this context is the Convention on the Rights of the Child, a pivotal international treaty that underscores the child's entitlement to a range of fundamental rights. These rights encompass the child's right to life, liberty, and the pursuit of an adequate standard of living. Moreover, they encompass access to essential healthcare, education, opportunities for recreation and play, psychological well-being, and, crucially, the right to live in an environment characterized by peace and security.

It is disheartening to note that, despite the global recognition of these rights, Palestinian children continue to endure adverse circumstances and challenges that impede their development and well-being. This underscores the urgent need for sustained efforts to uphold and protect the rights of these vulnerable children, ensuring they have the opportunity to flourish in an environment conducive to their physical, mental, and emotional growth.

The deliberate targeting and tragic loss of Palestinian children's lives (illustrated in table 1) has been a persistent policy attributed to the Israeli political and military leadership. This policy has resulted in a distressing number of child casualties, with Palestinian children bearing the brunt of the suffering, notably during the 2014 conflict. According to reputable human rights organizations and United Nations reports, the Israeli forces caused the deaths of at least 2,251 individuals during the July-August 2014 conflict. As mentioned earlier, among these casualties, 551 to 578 were innocent children, and an additional 3,374 children sustained injuries. It is important to note that the exact figures may vary depending on the reporting source.

Table 1

PALESTINIAN CHILDREN KILLED BY ISRAELI FORCES FROM 2000-2022

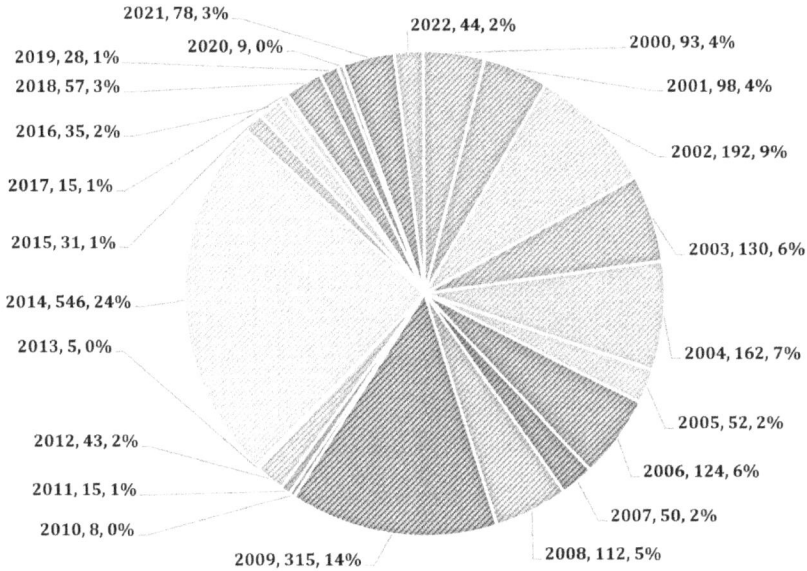

2021, 78, 3%
2022, 44, 2%
2019, 28, 1%
2020, 9, 0%
2000, 93, 4%
2018, 57, 3%
2001, 98, 4%
2016, 35, 2%
2002, 192, 9%
2017, 15, 1%
2015, 31, 1%
2003, 130, 6%
2014, 546, 24%
2013, 5, 0%
2004, 162, 7%
2005, 52, 2%
2012, 43, 2%
2006, 124, 6%
2011, 15, 1%
2007, 50, 2%
2010, 8, 0%
2009, 315, 14%
2008, 112, 5%

Source: Essential Statistics. (n.d.). Defense for Children Palestine. Retrieved October 4, 2023, from https://www.dci-palestine.org/essential_statistics

Further documented evidence from the human rights organization Defense for Children Palestine reveals that since the onset of the Al-Aqsa Intifada in 2000, a total of 2,270 Palestinian children have tragically lost their lives due to actions by the Israeli occupation army (up until May 1, 2023). Shockingly, of these victims, 546 were Palestinian children who met their untimely demise in 2014. These tragic incidents were primarily concentrated during Israeli military operations in the Gaza Strip. Examples of these heartbreaking occurrences include the abduction and subsequent murder of the Jerusalemite child, Muhammad Abu Khudair, by settlers; the heinous attack on the Dawabsha family in Duma village, leading to their fatalities; and the heart-wrenching case of Muhammad Haitham

Al-Tamimi, a two-and-a-half-year-old from Nabi Saleh, who was tragically targeted by an occupation soldier's sniper while he and his father were in their yard in June 2023. In general, most instances of child casualties are primarily linked to Israeli military actions, the presence of war remnants and landmines, particularly in Gaza, and the violence perpetrated by occupation soldiers and settlers in the West Bank.

Another devastating incident involved the loss of three young lives, Khaled Bassam Mahmoud Saeed (13 years old), Abdel Hamid Muhammad Abdel Aziz Abu Zaher (13 years old), and Muhammad Ibrahim Abdullah Al-Satri (13 years old), who were killed by an Israeli drone missile strike northeast of Khan Yunis. The indiscriminate bombing by occupation tanks in 2001 also claimed the life of an infant, Iman Hajjo, during the random bombardment of Khan Yunis. The tragic case of Muhammad al-Durra, who was targeted by occupation soldiers while sheltering in his father's arms on Salah al-Din Street in the Gaza Strip in 2000, remains etched in memory.

During the Israeli occupation forces' aggression on the Gaza Strip in May 2021, which persisted for 11 days, Palestinian children were disproportionately affected. Approximately 72 children lost their lives due to Israeli warplanes bombing their homes, resulting in the complete annihilation of some families, including men, women, and children, such as the Abu Hatab, Abu Auf, Ashkentna, and Qalq families. What was documented by Defense for Children Palestine Branch regarding the number of Palestinian children killed can be reviewed in the following table[54].

---

[54] Essential Statistics, n.d.

Table 2

Palestinian Children Killed 2014–2018

				Cause of death				
Year	Clashes	Air & ground attacks	During assassination attempts	Gunfire opened randomly	Closures	Unexploded ordnance	Other	Total
2014	9	380	150	5	0	1	1	546
2015	8	1	0	9	0	0	13	31
2016	6	2	0	3	0	0	24	35
2017	7	2	0	0	0	1	5	15
2018	21	2	0	0	0	0	0	23
Total:								650

The above table (Table 2) reflects the causes of death for Palestinian children killed by Israeli settlers and forces in the Occupied Palestinian Territory from 2014 to 2018, according to DCIP's documentation.[55]

---

[55] "July 22 Update," DCIP, 2014, paras. 3-7.

Table 3

PALESTINIAN CHILDREN INJURED BY ISRAELI FORCES FROM 2008-2022

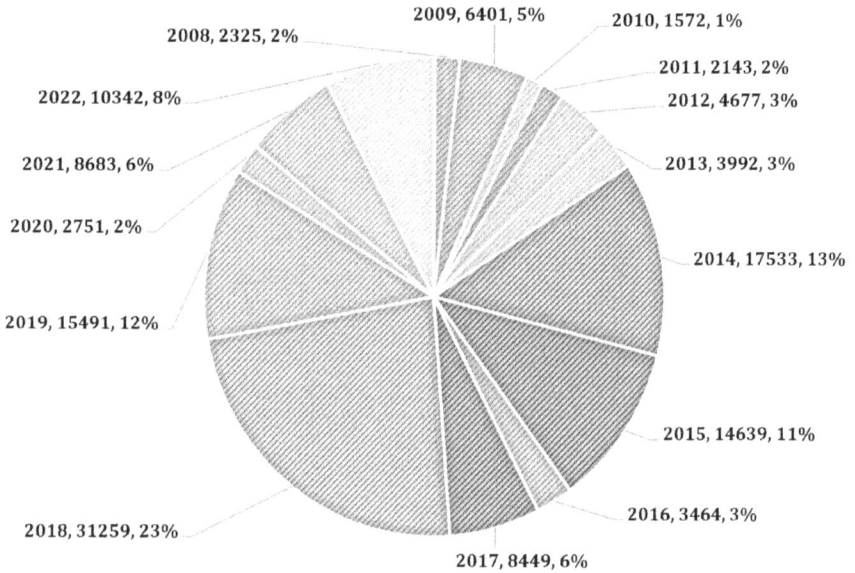

2008, 2325, 2%
2009, 6401, 5%
2010, 1572, 1%
2011, 2143, 2%
2012, 4677, 3%
2013, 3992, 3%
2014, 17533, 13%
2015, 14639, 11%
2016, 3464, 3%
2017, 8449, 6%
2018, 31259, 23%
2019, 15491, 12%
2020, 2751, 2%
2021, 8683, 6%
2022, 10342, 8%

Source:

الأطفال الفلسطينيون تحت الاحتلال | مركز المعلومات الوطني الفلسطيني

.(n.d.). Info.wafa.ps. Retrieved October 4, 2023, from
https://info.wafa.ps/ar_page.aspx?id=y7SojLa9133973541ay7SojL.

The data presented in the table 3 from the Palestinian Wounded Foundation reveals that during the first intifada spanning from 1987 to 1993, more than 70,000 individuals were wounded, with a significant portion being children. Distressingly, approximately 40% of these individuals continue to grapple with permanent disabilities. Among the long-term consequences, 65% experience conditions such as cerebral palsy, hemiplegia (paralysis of one side of the body), or paralysis of limbs, some of which have necessitated limb amputations. Moving on to the Al-Aqsa Intifada, which transpired from September 29, 2000, to the end of December

2007, data from the Palestinian Central Bureau of Statistics indicates that there were 31,873 reported injuries. For the period from 2008 to April 2022, encompassing both adults and children who sustained injuries, information gathered from the United Nations Office for the Coordination of Humanitarian Affairs in the Occupied Palestinian Territory, as well as human rights institutions and centers[56].

Table 4

PALESTINIAN CHILDREN INJURED BY ISRAELI FORCES BY REGION FROM 2000-2022

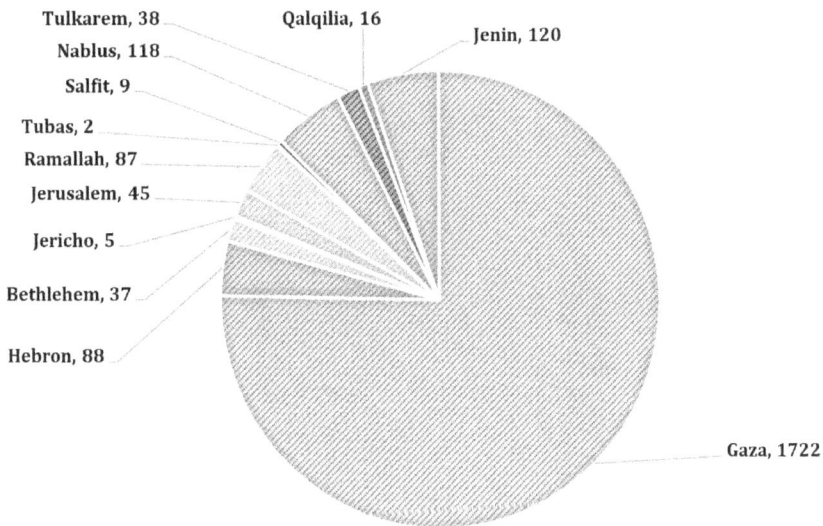

Tulkarem, 38; Qalqilia, 16; Jenin, 120; Nablus, 118; Salfit, 9; Tubas, 2; Ramallah, 87; Jerusalem, 45; Jericho, 5; Bethlehem, 37; Hebron, 88; Gaza, 1722

Source: Essential Statistics. (n.d.). Defense for Children Palestine. Retrieved October 4, 2023, from https://www.dci-palestine.org/essential_statistics

The data presented in the table 4 illustrates a significant rise in the number of injured in the Gaza Strip during various periods, including the Israeli aggression of 2014, the "return marches" from March 30th

56 الأطفال الفلسطينيون تحت الاحتلال | مركز المعلومات الوطني الفلسطيني, n.d.

to November 1st, 2018, and the Gaza war in May 2021. As for the West Bank, December 2017 stands out as a month with the highest number of casualties, with approximately 5,400 individuals injured during protests against US President Trump's decision to recognize Jerusalem as the capital of the occupying state. This was followed by July 2017, during which approximately 1,400 individuals were injured due to protests against the installation of electronic gates at the entrances to Al-Aqsa Mosque by occupation authorities. These substantial casualty figures serve as a concerning indicator, suggesting that Israeli occupation actions continue to jeopardize the well-being of Palestinian children and civilians[57].

Table 5

THE AVERAGE NUMBER OF PALESTINIAN CHILDREN IMPRISONED BY ISRAELI FORCES FROM 2008-2022

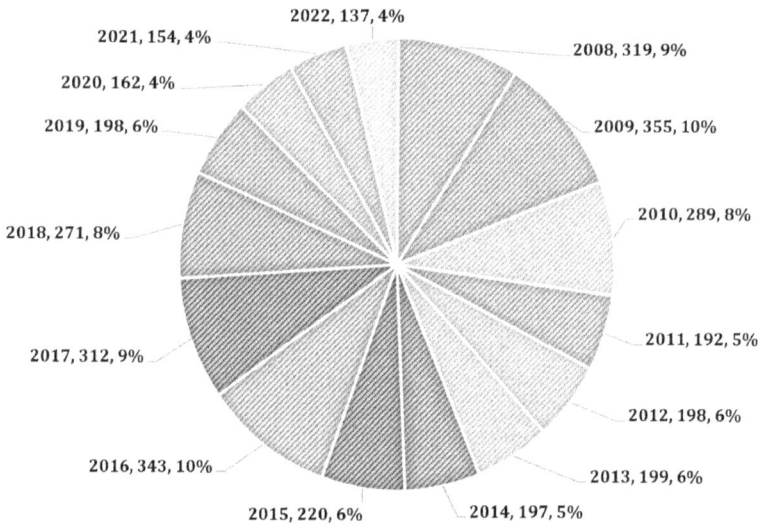

Source:
الأطفال الفلسطينيون تحت الاحتلال | مركز المعلومات الوطني الفلسطيني

. (n.d.). Info.wafa.ps. Retrieved October 4, 2023, from https://info.
wafa.ps/ar_page.aspx?id=y7SojLa9133973541ay7SojL

---

[57] **n.d.**, الأطفال الفلسطينيون تحت الاحتلال | مركز المعلومات الوطني الفلسطيني

The data presented in the table 5 shows that since 1967, Israeli authorities occupying Palestinian territories have detained approximately 50,000 Palestinian children, with around 20,000 of them apprehended since the start of the Al-Aqsa Intifada on September 28, 2000. Among these, 9,000 children were detained during the period known as the "October Ignition" in 2000. As of October 1, 2015, these detentions accounted for 20% of all arrests during that time frame, with a significant portion originating from Occupied Jerusalem.

In the year 2022 alone, Israeli occupation arrested roughly 770 children, and as of April 17, 2023, approximately 160 children remain in Israeli detention centers. These statistics highlight the substantial number of Palestinian children subjected to arrest and detention by the occupying Israeli forces, particularly in the context of the Al-Aqsa Intifada and its aftermath.[58]

The Palestinian Ministry of Health documented a significant toll on the well-being of Palestinians during the conflict in the Gaza Strip from July 7th to August 26th, 2014.[59] Their report indicates that a staggering 11,100 individuals were wounded during this period, with a distressing 3,374 of them being children. According to estimates by the United Nations, around 1,000 of these children are expected to bear permanent disabilities for the remainder of their lives due to the injuries sustained in the war.[60]

These injuries have left a lasting impact on the physical appearance of those affected. The range of injuries suffered by participants in this study varied widely, encompassing limb loss, eye impairments, significant organ damage, and the enduring presence of bomb shrapnel embedded throughout their bodies.[61] Additionally, participants reported a multitude of dermatological issues, including rashes, scars, eye problems, muscle aches, sores, and chronic pain. These findings highlight the profound psychological and physical challenges faced by those affected by the conflict.

---

[58] الأطفال الفلسطينيون تحت الاحتلال | مركز المعلومات الوطني الفلسطيني, n.d.

[59] IMEU, 2014 Sept.

[60] UN, 2014b.

[61] UN, 2014b.

Al Jazeera reported some of the victims' stories, like Amir Ibrahim Al Reqeb, 9 years old from Khan Yunis:

> July, on the first night of Eid al-Fitr, an Israeli attack hit near Amir's home in the town of Bani Suhaila, in Khan Yunis, in the southern part of the Gaza Strip.
>
> His uncle and two of his neighbors were killed in the attack. Thirty-seven others were injured, including Amir.
>
> First responders could not find Amir easily. They thought he was dead, but later found his body about 100 meters away, covered in sand.
>
> "Amir suffered an injury to his skull and broken bones in his jaw," his mother, Ibtisam, recalls. She then pointed to the shrapnel that injured Amir in different parts of his body, particularly his eye and his lungs. "He lost one of his eyes," she continued in a muffled voice.
>
> Since the war, Amir has become a permanent visitor to hospitals. He endured a series of surgeries in both Israel and the West Bank and spent six months in the ICU, which forced which forced him to leave school.[62]

At 38 years old, Ibtisam dedicated herself entirely to caring for Amir. She made the difficult decision to leave her newborn, who coincidentally arrived on the same day as Amir's injury, July 27, 2014. She stood by Amir's side, even as he was transferred to an Israeli hospital just three days after the incident. Among the casualties was Muntaser Bakr, a 14-year-old from Gaza City:

> At 11, Muntaser witnessed one of the most horrific scenes a minor can experience. In one of the most controversial Israeli attacks during the war, Muntaser and seven of his relatives and friends,

---

[62] Al-Haddad, 2017, "Muntaser Bakr," para. 1-4.

mostly minors, became the targets of Israeli missiles, while they were playing football on the beach.

Muntaser and three other children from his extended family managed to escape wounded, but four others, including his brother, were killed in the attack.

Three days after the tragedy, Muntaser awoke from a coma and started shouting: "They're all dead! I killed them, I killed them." He clung to his mother with both hands, before she said: "You did not kill anyone." [63]

---

[63] Al-Haddad, 2017, "Muntaser Bakr," para. 1-4.

CHAPTER 2:

"Destruction was everywhere"

Survivors who were displaced due to the Israeli bombings faced not only severe physical injuries that were life-threatening but also endured profound emotional and psychological consequences. These included the loss of loved ones, including children and family members, as well as displacement from their homes, which compelled them to repeatedly seek new safe havens to evade ongoing bombardments. Schools were repurposed as overcrowded shelters, which provided limited respite but gave rise to additional challenges.

The U.N. Office for the Coordination of Humanitarian Affairs reported that the war destroyed the homes and the livelihoods of the Palestinian people in the Gaza Strip. As a result of Operation Cast Lead,

> in 2014, Gaza witnessed the highest rate of internal displacement since 1967, as a result of the July-August hostilities. From previous hostilities, UNRWA had anticipated sheltering a maximum 50,000 internally displaced persons (IDPs) in its installations, but the eventual peak number was almost six times higher. Almost 500,000 people, 28% of the population, were internally displaced at the height of hostilities in UNRWA schools, government and informal shelters, and with host families. As of the end of December, an estimated 100,000 persons remain displaced throughout Gaza [64]

---

[64] UN OCHA, 2015a, p. 10.

Losing their home was the most devastating thing that could happen to those who survived. One mother talked about the impact that the loss of her home has had on her extended family, who has been separated. "We had to evacuate the house," she said. "We left without taking anything because we thought we were coming back." She was shocked when she heard that her home had been destroyed: "We lost everything." The family now mainly lives in a tent on the land where the house was. The woman worries about the future and worries about her children: "My oldest son wets his bed and my youngest daughter bites her nails and even when they're playing their father gets angry and so they can't play anymore."[65]Others were not so lucky. One mother recalls her family fleeing:

> During the war in 2014, I left with my ten children. It was horrifying. The Israelis had started their ground invasion. I had to jump fences with my family and there were helicopters overhead. I took all my children with me; my youngest was eight years old. We went to the UN school on foot and we were walking blindly from the fear. I could see the Israeli soldiers and the bombing was just random. The fear was indescribable.[66]

They are now living in a large tent-like structure that survived the bombing of the July-August 2014 war, but her nearby home is a pile of rubble. "The children's education has been very affected," she said. "They can't study because there is no space and there is no electricity and they can't study when it gets dark."[67]

For those who wish to establish a new life elsewhere, travel through the Erez Crossing, which is limited to what the Israeli military deems "exceptional humanitarian cases," such as medical emergencies, presents a nearly insurmountable challenge for Palestinians in Gaza seeking to with journey to other parts of the Occupied Palestinian Territories, or other parts of the world. In the early part of 2016, the daily average of Palestinians

---

[65] Ibid., p. 47.

[66] Ibid., p. 51.

[67] Rought-Brooks, 2015, p. 51.

crossing through Erez stood at approximately 500, a stark contrast to the over 24,000 who passed through daily in September 2000, just before the outbreak of the second Palestinian uprising, or "Intifada." The flow of goods to the other parts of the Occupied Palestinian Territories dwindled significantly, with only 15% of the pre-2007 closure levels recorded during the first ten months of 2016.

Furthermore, Israeli restrictions on the entry of construction materials into Gaza, coupled with a lack of funding, have obstructed the reconstruction of nearly 17,800 homes severely damaged or destroyed during Israel's 2014 offensive in Gaza. As a result, approximately 65,000 people remain without shelter.[68] Adding to this dire situation, Egypt has imposed stricter limitations on the movement of Palestinians and blocked regular freight traffic of goods at the Gaza border. In 2016, the Rafah border crossing with Egypt was mostly shut, only occasionally allowing passage for medical patients, visa holders (e.g., students and pilgrims to Mecca), and those holding foreign passports. The number of people crossing through Rafah plummeted drastically from an average of 40,000 per month in both directions during the first half of 2013 to just 3,196 per month in the first ten months of 2016.[69]

The Defense for Children International - Palestine (DCIP) has reported Israeli practices collective punishment against Gaza's Palestinian population, including denial of access to medical care, power, clean water, and the bombing and destruction of homes, which has resulted in the displacement of inhabitants.[70] Access to healthcare is another critical concern for Palestinian children in Gaza. The ongoing blockade has led to a shortage of medical supplies and equipment, affecting the quality of healthcare services. In addition, children who require specialized medical treatment not available in Gaza often face significant hurdles in obtaining permits to leave the territory for treatment. Gaza's children are particularly vulnerable to malnutrition and food insecurity due to the blockade, which limits the availability of essential food items. In a 2021 report, the World

---

[68] Human Rights Watch, 2017, p. 349.

[69] Human Rights Watch, 2017.

[70] DCIP, 2014.

Food Programme (WFP) noted that 68% of Gaza's population, including children, relied on humanitarian assistance to meet their basic food needs.[71]

Due to the massive life changes caused by the war, the psychological impact has spread to every aspect of family life, including the future of the remaining children. One woman said, "There is no work. I have four sons and they don't work and so they can't marry. They all live with me in one room."[72] Women in several focus groups talk about young people in Gaza looking to leave because there were no prospects. The blockade imposed by Israeli occupation, in collaboration with Egypt, has left nearly two million people living in the Gaza Strip with severely limited access to resources, education, healthcare, and job opportunities. The resulting despair has given rise to a sense of hopelessness among the youth, leading many to believe their dreams can only be realized by leaving Gaza.

The decision to leave is not made lightly. Young Gazans face significant challenges in their quest for a better life. They must navigate a complex web of restrictions and regulations, often relying on risky routes and smugglers to travel to destinations in Europe, the Middle East, or beyond. This journey includes many potential dangers, from exploitation to human trafficking, but it offers a glimmer of hope for those who are willing to take the risk.

The impact of young Gazans leaving on families, particularly on mothers, is profound. Mothers are often the pillars of strength in Gaza's tight-knit communities, and they invest immense love and hope in their children. When a young person decides to leave, it becomes suffering for the entire family. Mothers must grapple with a complex mix of emotions: their pride in their child's determination to seek a better life, the fear for their safety on the arduous journey, and the heartbreak of saying goodbye, possibly never seeing their child again. Mothers in Gaza also bear the practical consequences of their children's departure. They face constant worry for their children's safety when they embark on this uncertain journey. They fear for their well-being in unfamiliar lands, especially

---

[71] WFP, 2021.
[72] Ibid., p.54.

considering the language and cultural barriers they may encounter. These anxieties can take a toll on mothers' mental and emotional well-being. The absence of their sons and daughters leaves a void that can never be filled. These families lose not only a cherished member but also a potential source of financial support in a region where unemployment is widespread.

Additionally, the burden of maintaining a connection with their children abroad often falls on mothers, who must navigate the complex world of international communication and bureaucracy. Despite the pain and hardship associated with their children's departure, most mothers in Gaza support their children's dreams. It's a testament to the resilience and love of mothers that these women can let go and allow their children to chase their dreams. They hope their sacrifices will lead to better lives, far away from the harsh realities of life in Gaza, far away from the continuous suffering and war.

A recurring scenario among the participants I interviewed as part of this study was loss of family members, destruction of homes, and internal displacement, ongoing consequences that demanded constant treatment and attention. During the 2014 conflict, a significant number of individuals experienced displacement, with hundreds of thousands of people being uprooted from their homes. Despite the dedicated efforts of humanitarian organizations, the conflict posed a pervasive threat to the safety of the affected population. Regrettably, in 2014 three UNRWA shelters were inadvertently struck by Israeli forces, resulting in the tragic loss of 45 lives, including 17 children. Moreover, the protracted conflict and the accompanying blockade led to dire socio-economic consequences, with a staggering 70% of young individuals finding themselves without employment opportunities, and a striking 80% of the population becoming reliant on external aid for sustenance.

Currently, the conflict shows no signs of resolution, perpetuating a state of enduring uncertainty and instability. These multifaceted challenges have compounded the psychological distress and complex trauma that result from the long years of occupation and war and oppression, extinguishing prospects for a promising future or any semblance of stability. Though he and his sons survived, Wahdan knows that this is only the beginning of new suffering and further sorrow, as they all now must live with their injuries and their grief:

> As for my kids, they received treatment in Turkey. [He began to reveal the injuries of his children] This one has a fractured skull, this boy has bomb shrapnel in his face and was burned, and this one was burned. Also, the destruction of shrapnel is showing in this body, and others still have the bomb shrapnel in the body. These two were treated in Turkey, they stayed almost a month and they came back.
>
> Their mother was killed on the spot. They carried her body out of the house. She was dead on the spot.

The level of grief is incomprehensible, yet Wahdan, his sons, and other survivors had no choice but to accept what happened to them, even though the news was given to them a little at a time, to soften the blow:

> At the beginning, I thought that I am the only one who was injured, then I found out that my wife was killed and my kids were injured. Two of my nephews, they were 12 and 14 years old, two young daughters, my nieces, a little child aged two years old, and a little 4-year-old child were killed, as well.
>
> Twelve members of my family were all killed by the Israeli bombing. Eight of them were bombed while they were at home in Beit Hanoun. The house was bombed and completely totaled; three floors fell on them completely.
>
> We only found some of their body parts. We found nothing of my dad's body, we found my mother's hand, parts of my sister-in-law's body, and the kids, we found their legs only. Of the eight individuals in Beit Hanoun, we found 70 kilos.

After hearing this story, I prompted, "I would like to ask about you and your children's psychological situation."

"Until now," he replied, "we have not settled down, this son is staying at my brother's house. I cannot keep him with me and provide him the comfort he needs, because he is young and he needs special care. The psychological problems these children suffer from, I mean until today this son still urinates on himself, and at night sometimes screams, 'Rockets!'"

Wahdan has educational training that he applies to his misfortune, though that was not what he ever anticipated his training would be needed for. Unfortunately, not all Palestinian parents have this type of training:

> I am a teacher and I have an educational credential, which means I have some knowledge on how to deal with my child when he wakes up scared and screaming. I cuddle him, comfort him, and talk to him so he can forget. I understand them, what they have witnessed is unbearable.

> No matter what kind of a hard time he gives me I will never lay my hand on him, yell at him, or do anything wrong to him. I always keep in mind his difficult psychological situation.

Because of the bombings, after losing her house Um Fadi went from being a wife, mother, and homemaker in Gaza with a husband and healthy sons and daughters to a grieving, mentally unstable homeless woman shuffling between relatives' homes and improvised school shelters. Um Fadi spent time in the school shelters with her family. I asked her about her experience there. She said,

> Life was very difficult. We went to the Christian school. Three families stayed in one room. Many families were staying with us in the same school and other families were in other schools. Other women and I would meet and talk. However, If my son entered the room, the other women would get upset and they would fight about it.

> There is no place like home. In the school shelters, when you need water, there is no water. When you need electricity, there is no electricity. Sewage had flooded the area. There were no

showers, so we smelled. I met a woman who lived close to the school, and she offered for me and my daughters to go every now and then to shower at her house.

The road to recovery is long and seems hopeless for these displaced victims. They are still standing, still breathing, yet they have lost their lives. Um Fadi continued:

It caused me grief and a breakdown as we lost everything in a second. Till now, I feel sad and oppressed. I lost my house, and I live now in the street. I used to live in the middle of the city.

I sometimes remember what happened and cry. My children tell me to forget, and I tell them it's impossible as we saw lots of horrible things. I wish that I could have a house to get rid of the flies and mice. In addition, my daughters would have the chance to live normally as other girls.

Similarly, Asmaa has her own severe problems but still grieves for lost family:

I cannot see with my eye anymore. My body is full of shells and bomb shrapnel. But the most difficult thing is that my sister, her daughter, my sister-in-law were killed. I saw my brother-in-law's kids on fire after the shelling in front of my eyes. I tried to come closer to them, the steam was coming out of their bodies and all of them burned. I thank the Lord, they are better now. Their dad lost his limbs. Their mother was killed and the children received treatment in Turkey.

The young Wael and his son Sharif were seriously affected physically and psychologically after the Israeli army bombed their car. Wael spoke on the unimaginable tragedy he experienced:

On August 1, 2014, there was to be a truce. At 8 a.m. they bombed again, a very heavy bombardment. There was fear among the women and children. We decided to get out of the house to a safe place in the other half of the country.

My brother, my wife, my brother's wife, and all the children went to the center of the town and on the road about a thousand meters from the house. Three reconnaissance rockets landed on us. I was hit in my legs and my son was killed. My brother and his wife and sister were martyred and my daughter was burnt. And my sister, as well, has burns and shrapnel, and my nephew has burns and shrapnel.

I asked, "Was your wife with you?"

"Yes," Wael replied.

"What happened with her?"

"Her two legs were amputated."

I then talked with Wael about transitioning to being an able-bodied man to a man with a disability whose son also suffers the same disability.

Wael said, "I feel very scared. Fear of the future. I will not remain what I was."

"Does your fear of the future make you nervous?" I asked.

"Really. Sometimes, if I think about the future, I will have a nervous outburst at anyone in front of me. My nervousness and stress have increased. I easily get nervous and lonely and introverted, always worried and thinking about the future.

"I mean, if my friend called me out the door of the house, I get angry. I stayed outside the house for one, two or three hours because if I stay in the house, I will make problems with everyone."

Widespread bombings and acts of violence have resulted in a significant number of casualties, and survivors often have severe physical injuries. These survivors often lack the necessary medical and financial resources to provide adequate treatment for their injuries, a situation exemplified by Asmaa. Asmaa's tragic experience involved the loss of 12 family members while she was fleeing from the relentless bombardments with her youngest daughter. Unfortunately, she was unable to protect all her other children during this harrowing ordeal. Asmaa shared with me the nature of her own injuries, as well as those suffered by her family members:

> I, my two children, and my husband were injured. My husband was injured in the eyes and head. I was injured in the eyes and my body. My back was open from the injury and I have bomb fragments in my entire body.
>
> My son was injured in the eyes. My daughter was injured in her chest. She has no nipple in her breast anymore and shrapnel in her body and legs.
>
> I suffered a serious injury in my back and my eye. My entire body is full of shells and bomb shrapnel. Look and see, some of it still in my hand and my eye. My eye also has fragments in it and injured from the inside. My entire body is full of shells and bomb shrapnel.

As mentioned previously, Um Hani was shocked that Israelis directly attacked Palestinian citizens in their homes:

> We saw our relative who was martyred while he was walking with his mother, and she and his brother couldn't get back to him. His brother was with him, and he was unable to minister him. The shelling was above our heads and under us. If they tried to minister to the guy, he would have stayed alive, but he was martyred.

She described more of the immediate aftermath of bombings:

> Suddenly, I saw women running from the east side of Beit al-Sarsak. The women ran in their sleeping clothes. I believe that, instead of wearing their sleeping clothes and makeup, they should have themselves ready, because they know we are at war.
>
> My daughters and I slept in prayer clothes. Whoever became

too hot would take off their clothes and wrap them around their head; that way, in the case of an emergency, they could exit immediately.

These interviews were conducted to investigate the enduring psychological challenges and disturbances experienced by individuals following bombings and acts of violence. Presented below are firsthand narratives that shed light on the persistent psychological burdens faced by Palestinian families as they grapple with the aftermath of these traumatic events. Wa'd told me, "I lost most of my hair, it greatly affected me psychologically." Um Hani lost her son, her home, and her livelihood. Her husband was a paraplegic before the war, and now Um Hani suffers from her own serious injuries after being bombed. She recalled her last conversation with her son:

I stayed at the hospital for two days. The third day there was a truce for eight hours. During this time my son and his wife managed to visit me in hospital.

On that day we talked so much and I asked him about our home and our livelihood. He told me he didn't care about the war and the shelling, and always went to feed our animals and birds in the Juhor ad-Dik region. I told him to leave out the chickens and goats, feed them only and return. But he refused and told me, what the Lord wished will be done.

He went with his brother to the house. They fired F-16 missiles on the house. My brother called my sister who accompanied me to the hospital, asking her to check on the martyrs or wounded in the emergency [department] in the hospital.

My sister went quickly to the emergency department in the hospital and she forgot her mobile phone next to me. My brother called her again. When he heard my voice, he closed the phone in my face. He was afraid I would be shocked by the news.

In the hospital room, a woman next to me heard the news from the radio about the bombing of a Musalam house in

Abu Issa by an F-16. The houses were completely shelled and bulldozers demolished it. Destruction was everywhere and there is a wounded Hisham, and a missing Hossam.

I said this house is my house and these are my children. Because of the severity of pain and shock, my brother called the doctor and asked him to give me painkillers so that I can bear what happened. I stayed in the hospital for 17 days and they told me I have Hepatitis A. For 17 days I went without eating or drinking, only I survived on intravenous therapy (IV) fluid.

In addition to relaying accounts like these from adults like Um Hani, the purpose of this work is also to explore and give voice to the experience of Palestinian children who have survived war trauma, are victims of traumatic events due to war, and who continue to suffer and to cope with their experiences, all while trying to accept and understand what has happened to them. Pronounced and disturbing behavioral changes occurred in the children after the attacks. Many women spoke of children having nightmares linked to their experiences during the war. One woman said, "My son is nine years old and he shouts during nightmares. I've taken him to a psychologist, but he is still the same."[73] Another said, "During the war one of my sons became very violent and at school they always give me a note about his behavior." Another mother said, "My daughter is 12 years old and afraid to go to the bathroom. We were living in Shuja'iyya. When we were told to evacuate, we were running over dead bodies."[74] A woman from Rafah explained her children's situation:

I was pregnant and have young children. My youngest was two and a half years old and my oldest was eight years old … Now, any noise or bangs, it triggers their crying because of the war. They think another war is coming.[75]

---

[73] Ibid., p. 43.

[74] Rought-Brooks, 2015, p. 43.

[75] Ibid.

Others talked about their children wetting the bed in a way that had not happened before. A woman from Rafah said, "I have a son who is seven years old, and he never used to wet his bed, but now constantly wets his bed. I took him to someone, but nothing works." Another woman from Beit Hanoun explained, "I have a two-and-a-half-year-old daughter and she wets her bed. She won't go out and says she's afraid. When she hears fireworks, she will say that it is shooting."[76]

Schoolwork has also suffered due to the impact of the war, reported the mothers. The children have lost interest in school and education, and in their future, they said. Two women from Beit Hanoun expressed concern about their children's education. One said her 14-year-old son "was a top student but after the war he hasn't been doing well. He used to study very hard but now he hasn't been able to study much." Furthermore, the 2014 Israeli military attack on Gaza had severe implications for education, preventing almost half a million Palestinian children in Gaza from starting the new school year. The assault damaged 244 schools that require repair, including at least two kindergartens. Additionally, over 142,000 housing units were affected, with 9,117 completely destroyed and 5,417 severely damaged. Consequently, a homelessness crisis ensued, leaving 500,000 individuals displaced, with 75,000 remaining without shelter.[77]

The Israeli blockade, which has been in place since 2007, restricts the movement of people and goods, including educational materials, in and out of Gaza. As a result, children in Gaza face challenges in accessing quality education. The United Nations Relief and Works Agency for Palestine Refugees in the Near East (UNRWA) reported that overcrowded classrooms, inadequate facilities, and a shortage of teaching staff have hindered the learning process for Gaza's children. [78]

Another parent explained that her son was also now struggling at school. "My ten-year-old son was studious but now when it comes to

---

[76] Ibid.

[77] UNRWA, 2015.

[78] UNRWA, "Gaza in 2020: A Livelihoods Perspective," 2021.

the exams he sits and can't write anything. He's become very slow and forgetful."[79]At a focus group in Rafah, a 15-year-old girl spoke:

> I was one of the top students in class, but my level has taken some steps back and my sisters are also affected. It affected us, the last war. We used to be able to walk alone but now we have to walk with others to go to school because we're nervous.[80]

Daily behavior has also markedly changed in these children, according to their mothers.

One mother said:

> My children are still affected by it. My son is in fourth grade, he suffers from a psychological disorder—he is very aggressive, and we have taken him to the doctors, and he wets his bed. He tends to be isolated. I have a three-year-old daughter who used to bite her nails during the war and now it is impossible for them to grow. I try to put socks on her hands to stop her biting them. She would bite her nails down to the flesh.[81]

One father spoke about his children and shared similar concerns:

> I have a five-year-old daughter. She never left my side—whenever a bomb would fall, I started singing to distract her. After each bombing we would pull together and bring everyone together. My daughter is still in shock and has speech issues and I can't find treatment. There is a center for speech therapy, and I hope to be able to afford it.[82]

---

[79] Ibid., p. 44.

[80] Rought-Brooks, 2015, p. 44.

[81] Ibid.

[82] Ibid. p. 43.

Asmaa worries daily about her daughter:

My girl was impacted psychologically and emotionally. Anytime she hears the shooting or the shelling, she starts crying and screaming. She became a psycho. She urinates on herself. Psychologically, she is suffering from post-war trauma. She gets very scared every time she hears the sounds of the drones. She runs to hide.

Yazan is another child whose experience of being attacked has led to fear in his daily life. I asked him, "When you hear the sound of tanks and drones, do you get afraid?"

"Yes."

"Do you escape from it? Do you get afraid of the F16s? Why are you afraid?"

Yazan replied, "I flee because they will shoot me."

"Where do you flee and hide?"

"In the room." He pointed to a place of hiding.

"Do you lock the door? Do you keep the light on, or do you turn them off?"

"I turn them off," said Yazan.

"Why do you turn the lights off?"

"Because they will see me."

The Palestinian population living in the Gaza Strip, particularly children, has endured immense suffering and hardship due to the Israeli aggressive policies and wars that have plagued the region for decades. The Gaza Strip has witnessed several major conflicts between Palestinian militant groups and Israeli forces, such as the wars in 2008-2009, 2012, 2014 and 2021. In addition, the Israeli siege imposed on the people of the Gaza Strip since 2016 has paralyzed all aspects of life in Gaza and contributed significantly to the suffering of Palestinians living there, particularly children. A study conducted by the Gaza Community Mental Health Programme (GCMHP) focused on 1,323 Palestinian children residing in the Gaza Strip. The findings of this research paint a troubling picture of the experiences endured by these children. It was revealed that a staggering 74% of these young individuals had been exposed to incidents involving aggression directed at their families. Additionally, 38% of them had a close family member who was incarcerated.

Furthermore, a significant 88% of the children reported that their homes had been subjected to raids by Israeli army forces. Shockingly, 51% of the children shared that they had encountered physical abuse at the hands of Israeli soldiers. Another distressing study indicated that a substantial 52% to 77% of these children had witnessed the traumatic killing of other individuals. Nighttime raids by Israeli soldiers had been witnessed by 88% of them, and 30% had family members who had suffered injuries because of these incidents.

It is crucial to acknowledge that such patterns of Israeli aggression have immediate and profound consequences on various segments of the Palestinian population residing in the Gaza Strip, with children being particularly vulnerable due to their sensitivity and inability to cope with the traumatic effects. This sensitive population, comprising almost half of Gaza's population, faces unique challenges and vulnerabilities that demand attention and action from the international community. Many Palestinian children in the Gaza Strip have experienced displacement multiple times throughout their lives due to conflict and the destruction of their homes. This constant upheaval disrupts their education, emotional well-being, and overall development. Repeated exposure to war, violence, loss of loved ones, and displacement have severely affected children's mental health. According to a UNICEF report published in 2018, nearly 300,000 Palestinian children in Gaza required psychosocial support due to trauma from conflict-related events.[83]

The complex trauma endured by Palestinian children resulting from the long years of occupation and oppression not only victimized them immediately but also ensnares them in the aftermath. They are exposed to distressing events that significantly impede their social development

---

[83] UNICEF, "Gaza: 10 years, 10 facts," 2017.

and mental well-being, resulting in a range of cognitive, emotional, and heightened psychological challenges, including post-traumatic stress disorder (PTSD) and depression.[84]

The Israeli aggression against Palestinians, characterized by acts such as murder, physical abuse, bombings, destruction of homes, schools, hospitals, farms and factories, shelling of public institutions, arrests, and the deprivation of essential resources like water, food, and electricity, profoundly and negatively impact the lives of Palestinian children. Notions of security, protection, and care remain elusive, perpetuating an existence marked by fear, anxiety, and hunger. These harsh circumstances delay the personal growth of Palestinian children during their critical developmental stages, thereby leaving long-lasting consequences on their individual psyches and the broader Palestinian society.

Nighttime bombardments have understandably had a profoundly negative psychological impact on the 53% of the Palestinian population in Gaza who are children.[85] These children have experienced death, fear, anxiety, depression, and trauma, manifesting in psychological symptoms such as sleep disturbances, eating disorders, fear of darkness, bedwetting, withdrawal, concentration difficulties, and other neuroses.[86] Studies have indicated that exposure to political violence is a risk factor linked to childhood behavioral problems like aggression, social withdrawal, insecurity, and low self-esteem.[87]

The scale of aggression inflicted by Israelis on Palestinian children has taken a toll, impacting them physically, psychologically, emotionally, and cognitively. This is evident in the use of internationally banned weapons, including Dense Inert Metal Explosives (DIME), armor-piercing bombs, white phosphorous, mercury, aluminum, cobalt, and other harmful substances, causing both immediate and long-term health consequences.[88]

---

[84] Qouta, Punamäki, & El Sarraj, 2008.

[85] Khamis, 2015.

[86] Kostelny and Garbarino, 2001.

[87] Kostelny and Garbarino, 2001.

[88] Middle East Monitor, 2014.

Additionally, the deliberate use of sonic booms generated by Israeli jets breaking the sound barrier during nighttime has caused immense distress among Gaza's residents, particularly children. These sonic booms have disrupted children's sleep patterns, elicited uncontrollable fears, and resulted in a range of psychological issues, including social withdrawal, panic attacks, constant alertness, anxiety, poor concentration, stuttering, regressive behavior, ticks, and somatic problems.[89]

The detention of Palestinian children and their family members, combined with Israeli-imposed blockades by land, sea, and air on the Gaza Strip over the past 11 years, has had a profound impact on the mental health of Palestinian children. Arbitrary detentions, which include the arrest and humiliation of parents and siblings in front of children, nighttime rounding up and torture of Palestinian families and individuals, and the detention of children as young as 10 years old, have had detrimental effects on the psychological well-being of Palestinian children. Studies have shown that the majority of young children exposed to repeated war trauma exhibit severe post-traumatic profiles, putting their future adjustment at significant risk.[90]

---

[89] Qouta, Punamäki, Miller, & El Sarraj, 2008.

[90] The Feldman and Vengrober, 2011.

CHAPTER 3:

"Even now, I imagine Israeli war airplanes shelling us with rockets"

Children around the world, both historically and in contemporary times, have been profoundly affected by the ravages of war. These young individuals, who managed to survive amidst the chaos, often bear the scars of their experiences: physical displacement, abduction, familial separation, and coercion into military service. Even those who escape physical harm may carry the heavy burden of psychological trauma as a result of their harrowing ordeals.[91] This trauma is not to be taken lightly; it can have enduring consequences, potentially manifesting as mental health issues that demand ongoing treatment.[92]

Children who have survived wars, as well as other man-made disasters such as ethnic cleansing and political oppression, typically do not emerge from these calamities unscathed.[93] Rather, they may pay a steep psychological and emotional price, which can also manifest in their behavior. Research into the emotional, behavioral, and psychological impacts of war on children reveals striking parallels with the effects experienced by children who have survived natural disasters like floods, hurricanes, or earthquakes.

Despite the long and painful history of violent conflicts, ongoing research is dedicated to uncovering the full scope of war's impact on children, especially the psychological effects.[94] Children exposed to war,

---

[91] Summerfield, 1997.

[92] Arroyo & Eth, 1985.

[93] Wright et al., 1997.

[94] Boothby, 1992.

ethnic cleansing, political oppression, interpersonal violence, and forced displacement often bear the effects of these experiences for a considerable period. It remains uncertain whether the long-term consequences of such events will resemble those of single traumatic incidents, which tend to exhibit a greater capacity for recovery, or whether they will resemble the complex and diverse outcomes associated with chronic child maltreatment.[95]

Chronic child maltreatment encompasses the sustained and recurring pattern of abusive or neglectful conduct directed towards a child over an extended time frame. This form of child abuse entails repeated instances or an enduring atmosphere of harm, rather than isolated or sporadic acts of abuse or neglect. Chronic child maltreatment can manifest in various forms, including physical abuse (such as physical harm or beatings), emotional abuse (involving consistent belittlement, humiliation, or rejection), sexual abuse (inappropriate sexual contact or exposure to explicit materials), and neglect (the failure to provide essential care, supervision, or emotional support, including basic needs like food, shelter, medical care, or emotional nurturing). The repercussions of chronic child maltreatment can be severe and long-lasting, impacting a child's physical, emotional, and psychological well-being. This may give rise to a range of developmental, behavioral, and mental health issues, and in some instances, these effects can persist throughout a person's lifetime. "We are always talking about post-war trauma, and its consequences are greater than the trauma of the war itself," Dr. Kamal Qadih told me, "because when physical pain ends, emotional pain is opened. Khuza'a and its neighboring areas, which are close to the Israeli border, continue to suffer up to today from the continuing psychological trauma and from the continuous terror unleashed daily by the Israeli attacks on the local civilians, especially children who cannot bear the shooting and the sound of missiles."

Across the globe, a clear parallel can be drawn between the plight of children affected by war and those enduring other profound life-altering events.[96] Research on post-traumatic stress disorder (PTSD)

---

[95] Garrick, Morrow, Shalev, & Eth, 2001.

[96] Jensen, 1993.

underscores that children living in conflict-ridden regions consistently exhibit symptoms akin to PTSD. These symptoms encompass recurring and uncontrollable thoughts, vivid sensory images, and subtle behavioral shifts that may only become apparent in specific cases.[97] For instance, the repercussions of exposure to warfare can be discerned when children incorporate trauma themes into their playtime activities, daydreaming, storytelling, music preferences, and other daily pursuits. One mother who fled with her family to Gaza City from Khuza'a said:

> My son is 9 years old and he still recalls events from 2009 when he was four years old as well as the last war. He plays with Legos and he makes a shape of Al Zafer tower and brings it down— every day.[98]

Furthermore, the aftermath of a child's exposure to war can materialize as emotional avoidance, characterized by a diminished interest in life and a tendency towards antisocial behavior—a concern that has persisted since the Second World War. Furthermore, the aftermath of a child's exposure to war can materialize as emotional avoidance, characterized by a diminished interest in life and a tendency towards antisocial behavior, a concern that has persisted since the Second World War. A study conducted in 1980 by Fee involving 6,604 children from primary schools in Belfast. The findings were then compared with similar studies conducted in London and the Isle of Wight by Rutter and colleagues in 1970 and 1975.[99] The results indicated that Belfast school children exhibited significantly higher levels of antisocial behavior compared to their counterparts in London and the Isle of Wight.[100]

---

[97] Ahmad et al., 2000; Arroyo & Eth, 1985; Eisenbruch, 1991; Garrick et al., 2001; Nader et al., 1993; Nader, Pynoos, Fairbanks, & Frederick, 1990; Qouta & El Sarraj, 2004.

[98] Ibid.

[99] Named Isle of Wight, by Rutter, Tizard, Yule, Graham, and Whitmore, 1976.

[100] Jensen & Shaw, 1993.

Further investigations have illuminated the impact of traumatic incidents on Palestinian children. These children have endured three or more traumatic occurrences, either directly affecting them or their families, with an alarmingly high number of affected children.[101] Such traumatic events encompass humiliation experienced by 99% of children, exposure to the sounds of explosions and bombs affecting 97%, attendance at funerals of martyrs impacting 85%, and exposure to land or air shelling affecting 84%.[102] Consequently, a substantial 41% of these children grapple with the burdens of PTSD. [103]

Post-Traumatic Stress Disorder (PTSD)

Post-Traumatic Stress Disorder (PTSD) has gained significant recognition, primarily in the context of military personnel. However, in the Palestinian population, it has become evident that PTSD also affects a substantial portion of the populace, including children, who display a broad spectrum of PTSD symptoms and complications stemming from prolonged exposure to trauma. Research has indicated that the most prevalent manifestations of PTSD among children in Palestine encompass cognitive symptoms, experienced by 25% of affected children. These cognitive symptoms may manifest as difficulties falling asleep, preoccupation with reliving traumatic experiences, or persistent concerns about personal safety. Emotional symptoms are another common facet, afflicting 22% of children. These symptoms include feelings of isolation, recurring nightmares, heightened anxiety or tension, sadness, fearfulness, and instances of bedwetting. Social behavioral disorders, affecting 22% of children, manifest as rudeness, aggressive behavior, defiance towards teachers and parents, and a diminished capacity to engage in typical childhood activities and pastimes. Furthermore, academic behavioral issues were observed in 17% of affected children. These problems entail an inability to concentrate

---

[101] Altawil et al., 2008.

[102] Altawil et al., 2008 Jan.

[103] Altawil et al., 2008 Jan.

on studies, declining academic performance, inattentiveness in class, and disruptive conduct at school. Somatic symptoms, experienced by 14% of affected children, encompass physical complaints such as headaches, stomachaches, hypochondriacal concerns, and somatic manifestations of distress. In summary, PTSD is a significant concern for a considerable segment of the Palestinian population, especially among children, where it manifests through cognitive, emotional, social, academic, and somatic symptoms. Understanding and addressing these manifestations are crucial for the well-being of affected individuals.[104]

PTSD Variables

Post-Traumatic Stress Disorder (PTSD) is a condition characterized by varying degrees of symptoms that can be influenced by factors such as gender, geographic location, and the level of treatment required. In a study conducted among adolescents aged 10 to 19, the Gaza Community Mental Health Programme (GCMHP) found that a significant proportion of these young individuals were grappling with PTSD. Specifically, the results revealed that 32.7% of the participants were experiencing severe PTSD symptoms, while 49.2% exhibited moderate symptoms, and 15.6% displayed mild symptoms. Only a small minority, 2.5%, reported no PTSD symptoms at all.

Further analysis of the data unveiled some noteworthy trends. Among the adolescents surveyed, boys appeared to be more susceptible to PTSD, with 58% of them exhibiting symptoms, in contrast to 42% of girls. Additionally, the study identified a significant discrepancy based on the living environment, with those residing in camps being disproportionately affected compared to their counterparts in towns. An overwhelming 84.1% of adolescents in camp settings reported experiencing PTSD symptoms, while only 15.8% of those in town areas displayed similar symptoms.[105]

---

[104] Altawil et al., 2008.

[105] GCMHP; Qouta, 2000.

These findings underscore the importance of considering various demographic and environmental factors when addressing the prevalence of PTSD among young individuals. Such insights can be invaluable in tailoring effective interventions and support systems to mitigate the impact of trauma in these communities.

Causes and Levels of PTSD

Individuals living in close proximity to areas affected by war often endure significant psychological trauma, especially children, who are particularly vulnerable to the adverse effects of conflict. Numerous studies, including research conducted by the Gaza Community Mental Health Programme (GCMHP), have shed light on the harrowing experiences of children in conflict zones. These experiences include witnessing funerals (reported by 95% of children), observing shootings (83%), encountering injured or deceased strangers (67%), and family members who were injured or killed (62%).[106]

For children residing in areas subjected to bombardment, the impact on their mental well-being is starkly evident. A staggering 54% of these children suffer from severe levels of PTSD, with 33.5% experiencing moderate levels, and 11% grappling with mild to doubtful levels of PTSD.[107] The enduring conflict in the Gaza Strip has left an indelible mark on Palestinian children, subjecting them to chronic violence, the loss of loved ones, the destruction of their homes and schools, and an ongoing atmosphere of insecurity. Over the past six decades, Palestinian children in Gaza have been exposed to a litany of traumatic events, including the loss of thousands of lives, widespread injuries, the partial or complete destruction of buildings, home demolitions, and the taking of prisoners by Israel.[108]One poignant example from 2014 underscores the extreme

---

[106] Murthy, 2007.

[107] Qouta & El Sarraj, 2002; Ran et al., 2010; Thabet, Tawahina, El Sarraj, & Vostanis, 2008; Thabet & Vostanis, 2011.

[108] Altawil et al., 2008; Barsella, 2006.

challenges faced by these children: a 16-year-old Palestinian named Ahmad Abu Raida was held hostage by Israeli soldiers and used as a human shield for a harrowing five-day ordeal near his residence in Khan Yunis.[109]

Clinical psychologists working in the region have witnessed a disturbing rise in psychological and behavioral issues among Palestinian children. These problems encompass not only PTSD but also anxiety, depression, speech impediments, aggressive behavior, sleep disturbances, difficulties in school, and bedwetting.[110] The cumulative toll of these traumatic experiences on the mental health of Palestinian children in Gaza is a matter of grave concern. Dr. Sami Owaida of the Gaza Community Mental Health Programme told me that every child in the Gaza Strip suffers from one or two symptoms of PTSD. Um Salah talked to me about the planes overhead scaring her and her children. I prompted: "Your children said that when they heard the sound of the reconnaissance plane or the F-16 they were afraid."

"I am really scared because of the sound," Um Salah said. "I remember what happened to us. My daughter always says to me, Mama there is the sound of a war plane. I tell her not to be scared, and my little son is scared and stays with me."

"What do they do when they feel afraid?" I asked.

"Normally they would be playing. Moayad comes rushing to put his head under the blanket and asks me if the war plane is flying or not. The girl is the one who fears more. 'Leave the game and stay with me until the warplane is gone,' I tell them.

"My daughter escapes to her room and closes the door on herself, and my youngest son runs and sits in my lap. My daughter, every day and at night, has unintentional urination.

"Moayad cries and shouts loudly, he is very nervous. Sometimes I become nervous, too."

Her daughter, Ghada, a six-year-old child, described her recurring fear of airplanes. "Do you feel afraid when you hear the sound of a warplane or reconnaissance aircraft?" I asked.

---

[109] Akram & Rudoren, 2014.

[110] Qouta, 2000.

"Yes," Ghada replied.

"Why are you afraid?"

"From the sound of the warplane."

"Do you have fear they are going to bomb you again?"

"Yes," said Ghada.

"What do you do when you are afraid?"

Ghada explained that she shut herself in her room.

"Do you also turn off the light?" I inquired.

"Yes, that is what I did."

"Why?"

"Because I'm afraid," responded Ghada.

"Are you afraid if they saw the light, they would bomb you again?"

"Yes."

Her brother Moayad shared the same intense fear. I asked him, "Do you feel afraid when you hear the sound of a warplane or reconnaissance aircraft?"

"I feel afraid they will bomb us again," said Moayad. "I put my head under the blanket until the plane goes."

Israeli airstrikes have had devastating consequences in densely populated urban areas, resulting in a significant loss of life and thousands of injuries.[111] This has raised concerns about the resulting profound health impacts. One alarming observation came from a hospital that reported a 60% increase in the proportion of children born with health defects. Additionally, there is growing concern that the use of depleted uranium in Israeli forces' ammunition may be linked to an increase in blood cancers.[112]

Beyond the immediate physical toll, the long-term psychological effects on young children are deeply distressing and appear inevitable. Research conducted over decades of conflict in Gaza consistently reveals a recurring pattern of psychological damage in children. [113] Traumatic experiences during various stages of the conflict have been shown to lead

---

[111] Zonszein, 2015.

[112] Zonszein, 2015.

[113] Summerfield, 1997.

to high levels of neuroticism and impairments in attention, concentration, and memory among Palestinian children in the Gaza Strip.[114]

Studies also suggest that cultural factors may play a role in the manifestation of anxiety and trauma-related disorders. For instance, a study found a notable occurrence (25%) of conversion fits, a type of functional neurological symptom disorder in Palestinian children exposed to traumatic events during the war. Cultural factors undoubtedly play a significant role in the manifestation of anxiety and trauma-related disorders among Palestinian children, especially in the context of prolonged conflict and exposure to traumatic events such as war. The unique cultural, social, and political landscape of Palestine shapes the experiences and responses of children to these adversities, influencing the presentation and prevalence of disorders like conversion fits (a type of functional neurological symptom disorder).

One crucial aspect of Palestinian culture that impacts the manifestation of anxiety and trauma-related disorders is the collective nature of society. Palestinian communities often place a strong emphasis on familial and communal ties, which can both provide a source of support and exacerbate stressors. In times of conflict and trauma, the entire community is affected, and children may internalize the collective trauma experienced by their families and communities. This collective trauma can manifest in various ways, including conversion fits. For instance, a study found a notable occurrence (25%) of conversion fits, a type of functional neurological symptom disorder in Palestinian children exposed to traumatic events during the war.[115] Moreover, the political context of Palestine, characterized by ongoing conflict and occupation, creates a pervasive sense of insecurity and instability. Palestinian children grow up in an environment marked by checkpoints, military incursions, and violence, which can lead to chronic stress and heightened anxiety levels.

---

[114] Qouta et al., 1995a.

[115] Hein, Qouta, Thabet, and El Sarraj, 1993.

The constant threat of harm and loss, coupled with limited resources and access to mental health services, further compound the risk of developing anxiety and trauma-related disorders.

Additionally, the lack of resources and infrastructure for mental health care in Palestine contributes to the challenges in addressing anxiety and trauma-related disorders among children. Limited access to trained mental health professionals and evidence-based treatments means that many children do not receive the support they need to cope with their experiences effectively.

Furthermore, there is evidence supporting a dose-effect relationship between cumulative trauma and PTSD symptoms. Children living in refugee camps north of Gaza City, who experienced relocation, disruptions in school life, and higher exposure to traumatic events like house demolitions, were at a higher risk of developing PTSD.[116] In the West Bank, Palestinian children primarily exhibited behavioral and psychosomatic problems, [117] with refugee camp residents experiencing more severe behavioral issues than those in villages or cities.

Even when violence temporarily ceased, the psychological suffering of children persisted. For example, a longitudinal study following the peace accord in 1993 found that the level of neuroticism in Gaza's Palestinian children decreased significantly after the accord. However, earlier exposure to traumatic events and nonacceptance of the treaty (continuing political conflict) predicted increased neuroticism and low self-esteem.[118]

A study involving 944 Palestinian children, aged between 10 and 19 years and without prior mental health issues, was conducted during the tumultuous last two and a half years of the Second Intifada. The research revealed that 32.7% of these children began experiencing acute symptoms of post-traumatic stress disorder (PTSD) necessitating psychological intervention, while 49.2% reported suffering from a moderate level of PTSD symptoms.

---

[116] Cf. Mollica, Poole, Son, Murray, and Tor, 1997.

[117] Baker, 1990.

[118] Qouta, Punamäki, and El Sarraj, 1995b.

The study identified several common traumatic experiences among the children, with the most prevalent being witnessing funerals (94.6%), witnessing shootings (83.2%), encountering injured or deceased individuals who were not relatives (66.9%), and witnessing family members being injured or killed (61.6%).

Furthermore, it was observed that 32.7% of children residing in community areas experienced acute PTSD symptoms, while simultaneously 49.2% of them reported moderate PTSD symptoms. Additionally, 15.6% of children experienced low levels of PTSD symptoms.[119]

According to the Diagnostic and Statistical Manual of Mental Disorders (DSM-5), Post-Traumatic Stress Disorder (PTSD) can be diagnosed in children who have experienced traumatic events associated with war or war-related circumstances. The diagnostic criteria for PTSD in children closely resemble those applied to adults. To receive a PTSD diagnosis, a child must have encountered a traumatic event involving exposure to death, severe injury, or sexual violence. This diagnosis is warranted if the distressing symptoms persist for at least one month following the traumatic incident, although sometimes these symptoms may not manifest until several months or even years later. The criteria for diagnosing PTSD can be categorized into three groups: (a) re-experiencing the trauma, which involves reliving the traumatic event through distressing and intrusive recollections, flashbacks, and nightmares, whether during sleep or during waking hours; (b) emotional numbness and avoidance, where children may display emotional detachment and avoidance behaviors. This can include avoiding reminders of the traumatic event, places associated with it, or people who evoke those distressing memories.

---

[119] Qouta and El Sarraj, 2004.

There may also be a diminished interest in activities and life in general; and (c) heightened arousal of the nervous system. PTSD can lead to increased arousal of the nervous system. This is marked by issues like sleep disturbances, irritability, difficulty concentrating, excessive vigilance, a constant sense of being on edge, and a heightened propensity for irritation and anger.[120]

The World Health Organization estimated that after the 2014 offensive, up to 20% of Gaza's population may have developed mental health conditions.[121] These statistics underscore the urgent need for comprehensive mental health support and intervention in the region to address the deep and lasting psychological wounds inflicted by prolonged conflict.

Subsequently, all participants showed at least a few or more of these signs and/or clinically significant PTSD symptoms. Some or all behavioral, cognitive, emotional, and physical signs and symptoms displayed or communicated by the participants and their parents during the interview or reported by the GCMHP are listed in Table 6.

---

[120] APA, 2013.

[121] World Health Organization, 2014.

Table 6
PTSD Symptoms

Behavioral signs	Cognitive signs	Emotional signs	Physical signs
Crying Difficulties staying still and in one place Recklessness Difficulties complying with rules at home Daydreaming Social withdrawal Wetting the bed Fear of darkness General tension Flashbacks Nightmares Avoidance behavior Difficulty sleeping Intrusive, distressing recollections of traumatic experiences	Confusion Lack of concentration Inattentiveness Incoherent speech pattern Deterioration in ability to achieve at school	Anxiety Sadness Fear and worry Stress Depression Irritability Hopelessness Crying and screaming Phobias related to the war experience Anxiety about health Feeling of insecurity Extreme sensitivity to fear of unknown Fear of the future Restlessness Fear of instability	Scars, wounds Missile splinters and fragments all over body Loss of limbs Loss of eyesight Excessive sweating Muscle pain General fatigue Headache Poor vision Muscle pain in chest Hypersensitivity to heart rate Difficulty swallowing, lump in throat Swelling Vomiting Diarrhea or constipation Inability to breathe

Some of the participants' typical comments were:

"I am aware that I still have a lot of feelings and bad memories about it, but I didn't deal with them."
"When I hear the sound of the tanks, the drones, or F-16s, I flee because it shoots me."
"I cannot stop thinking about it."

Most participants reported arousal symptoms - the continued reminders of the war caused them to have physical responses, such as sweating, breathing problems, headache, muscle pain or heart pounding:

"I felt irritable and angry."
"I felt on guard."
"I am scared all the time."
"I worry about what is going to happen next."
"I do not feel safe."
"I had trouble concentrating."
"I avoid talking about my feelings."

Despite efforts to avoid them, intrusive images and thoughts recurred:

"I keep thinking about it."
"I remember my mother, and I keep crying."
"Any reminder of my mother brought back feelings about it."
"I had dreams about it."
"The pictures about it cannot leave my mind."

The findings reported here align with existing research on the psychological impact of war trauma, specifically highlighting the connection between negative emotional and psychological symptoms in children who have experienced conflict. [122] This study confirms the presence of

---

[122] De Jong, Mulhern, Ford, Van Der Kam, & Kleber, 2000; El-Sarraj & Qouta, 2005;

Post-Traumatic Stress Disorder (PTSD) in Palestinian children as a result of their exposure to Israeli military violence, corroborating previous research.

In another study, researchers examined 121 Palestinian children, aged 6 to 16, residing in the Gaza Strip, where they assessed the prevalence and factors contributing to PTSD. This group consisted of 45% girls and 55% boys. The children were asked about their exposure to military violence, including personal experiences as targets of violence or witnessing violence directed at others, including family members. Additionally, they reported symptoms associated with PTSD, such as hypervigilance, avoidance behaviors, and intrusive thoughts. [123]

The study's outcomes are revealed that 33.5% of the children experienced moderate PTSD, while 11% exhibited mild to doubtful levels of PTSD symptoms.[124] Additional investigations of Palestinian children in the Gaza Strip, particularly those of primary school age, who have endured the consequences of war, have shown similarly high rates of PTSD reactions.

Based on the children's own reports, an alarming 72% of them exhibited PTSD reactions of at least mild severity, while 39% displayed moderate to severe reactions.[125] This consistent pattern underscores the profound psychological toll on the mental health of the Palestinian population from prolonged complex continuous trauma resulting from 75 years of occupation and oppression.[126] The diverse and long-lasting effects of extended and recurring trauma are distinctly different from the consequences of a single traumatic incident. Palestinian children are continuously experiencing prolonged and repetitive trauma, 24/7 confined, stuck, and under the blockade, with nowhere to go, getting subjected to unjust Israeli polices, bombing and drones. This traumatic experience environment that has existed in Palestine cannot be defined as PTSD

Garbarino et al., 1991b; Kinzie et al., 1996; Murthy & Lakshminarayana, 2006; Smith, Perrin, Yule, Hacam, & Stuvland, 2002; Thabet & Vostanis, 2000.

[123] Qouta, Punamäki, and El Sarraj, 2003.

[124] Qouta, Punamäki, and El Sarraj, 2003.

[125] Hein et al., 1993.

[126] Charara et al., 2017.

nor as Continuous Traumatic Stress Disorder only. It can be described as Complex Continuous Traumatic Stress Disorder because it has existed for over 75 years and has repeatedly impacted generations of Palestinian children.

In a personal interview, Akram Nafi, a psychiatrist from the GCMHP, argued that "in normal environments, the ideal solution would be to remove the cause of the problem; however, in Gaza, you can't change the situation. The solution would be to offer them a secure area for these children, but we can't offer that." Some have argued that there is no "post" in posttraumatic stress disorder for Palestinians in Gaza; the trauma is ongoing, with the ongoing blockade and violence.[127] PTSD shows up in children and parents to varying degrees, as described by the participants in the study. Um Fadi told me, "I became unable to sleep and nervous. I suffer from fatigue and am always unable to bear my children or husband." Similarly, Asmaa related her struggle to care for her traumatized daughter.

"Tell me about your psychological situation," I requested. "You told me your daughter urinates on herself and is always in fear. If she hears any sounds, she starts screaming. How do you deal with her situation?"

"My daughter becomes afraid of anything," Asmaa replied. "Yesterday, the kids in the neighborhood told her that the Israelis will come to take your mother, so my daughter started screaming. I start hugging her and mothering her, and I tell her that the kids are lying to you, there are no Israelis coming to take me.

"My girl became a psycho, every time she hears the word 'Israelis' she starts hiding, crying, and screaming. I start hugging her and mothering her, and I tell her the Israelis are gone, do not be afraid.

"Are you taking her to a psychologist?" I asked.

"Until now I did not take her because I am going to treatment for my eye. I have to have surgery. My eye is ruined from the inside, they told me it is going to cost $1,000. I will see after I take care of my eye because it has a bomb fragment.

"Then I will take care of my daughter, but the doctor told me not to worry, she will be okay. She also needs surgery on her chest, but they

---

[127] Charara et al., 2017.

told me to wait until she is 12 years old."

In the following sections, we will hear from more interview participants regarding both adults' and children's manifestations of trauma.

Anxiety

Many participants or their parents have reported experiencing symptoms of anxiety. Studies reported that Palestinian children living near the buffer zones with the Israeli occupation develop anxiety, deep fear, nightmares, and bed-wetting. These symptoms are believed to result from their exposure to violence and Israeli incursions in the area.[128] Importantly, these studies have highlighted a significant correlation between the prevalence of anxiety disorders and aggressive behavior in Palestinian children.

The psychological symptoms described by participants are diverse and encompass a wide range of emotional and cognitive experiences. These include a pervasive sense of general tension, health-related anxieties, academic difficulties, emotional instability, feelings of insecurity, restlessness, heightened sensitivity, excitement, and fear of the unknown and future, as well as episodes of depression. Moreover, many children have reported experiencing a decline in their academic performance because of these psychological burdens.

In addition to the psychological symptoms, physical complaints have also been noted. Palestinian children exposed to these distressing circumstances have reported various physical manifestations of their anxiety, such as chest muscle pain, breathing difficulties, heightened heart rate sensitivity, indigestion, swallowing difficulties, the sensation of a lump in the throat, swelling, diarrhea, constipation, colic, and vomiting episodes. Muscular pain affecting the limbs, back, and neck, as well as persistent fatigue, physical exhaustion, unsteadiness, and shivering, have been prevalent complaints among these children. Symptoms related to the urinary system, including bed-wetting and frequent urination, have also been observed.

---

[128] Charara et al., 2017.

Furthermore, a specific study involving Palestinian children has highlighted their responses to danger and life-threatening situations, which often include symptoms such as anxiety, somatization (physical symptoms without apparent medical cause), and withdrawal. Notably, younger children may exhibit regression into earlier stages of development when faced with such stressors. Almost all children in these circumstances tend to react with excessive fear, disturbances in sleep patterns, and increased dependence on their parents for emotional support.[129]

It is worth noting that there may be cultural variations in how anxiety and trauma-related disorders are presented and experienced among Palestinian children, suggesting the need for culturally sensitive approaches when addressing these issues. These findings underscore the profound impact of the challenging living conditions on the psychological and physical well-being of Palestinian children zones with living near buffer zones with the Israeli occupation, calling for urgent attention and support in the realm of mental health and psychosocial interventions.[130] Prolonged exposure to violence, uncertainty, and lack of access to basic necessities such as clean water, adequate food, and healthcare exacerbate Palestinian children's stress and anxiety. Some common symptoms of anxiety in Palestinian children that we found in our study include:

Excessive Worry: Many of the children I interviewed experienced excessive worry about various aspects of their lives, such as school, family, or their community's safety, and constant fear about their safety and the safety of their loved ones. The sound of explosions and sirens can be particularly distressing. The Israeli drones that fly over Gaza 24/7 significantly increase the anxiety level among Palestinian children. The message I kept getting from the children and their parents is, "We want to live in peace." This led me to produce a documentary interviewing Palestinian children, telling their stories, and giving them the chance to talk about their traumatic experiences and their dream of living in peace.

Irritability and Aggression: Anxiety can make children more irritable and prone to mood swings. Palestinian parents spoke about the

---

[129] Qouta et al., 2003, p. 226.
[130] Hein et al., 1993.

changes they have noticed in their children's behavior, and they become more irritable, prone to outbursts of anger, and have difficulty controlling their emotions. I cannot forget my interview with Wael and his son, Sharif. Sharif, who lost his mom, uncles, cousins, limbs, and eye, was very irritable and had anger outbursts at the other children at his home at the time of the interview. He was arguing, yelling at the other children, and asking them to leave his home.

Fears and Phobias: Many of the children develop specific fears or phobias related to their cultural or environmental circumstances, such as fear of political instability or violence. For example, Ragad expressed her anxiety about being able to protect her sister Maysa from any future wars. "What I keep thinking is that, the kids, I do not know what to do with them, should we take them and run away or what? I have no clue," she stated.

Tearfulness: The anxiety that Palestinian children experience leads to increased crying or emotional outbursts. A clear example of that was Ragad, who continuously cried throughout the interview as she was telling her family story and what they had to endure during the war.

Sleep Disturbances: Palestinian children and their parents spoke about sleep disturbances they have been experiencing such as nightmares, night sweats, and difficulty falling or staying asleep. Parents explained how their children become clingier and seek comfort at night and how some children also experience bedwetting.

Withdrawal: Some children experience withdrawal from social activities and isolate themselves from peers and family members. Children such as Yazan and Wa'ad, who experienced social withdrawal symptoms and night terrors, have lost all interest in activities they once enjoyed.

Difficulty Concentrating: Many children also experienced the inability to concentrate and perform well in school, leading to their decline in academic performance.

Regressive Behavior: Palestinian children also exhibit regressive behavior, such as bedwetting, clinging to their parents, and not wanting to leave their parents' side even to go and use the toilet.

When we address Palestinian children and their anxiety, it's essential to consider how the unique cultural and environmental factors, such as exposure to conflict and political instability, may contribute to their anxiety symptoms. These factors can add an extra layer of stress and trauma, potentially exacerbating anxiety.

In a separate research investigation involving Palestinian children ranging from 9 to 13 years of age, it was observed that they frequently exhibited anxiety-related issues. This finding is consistent with broader studies conducted on children living in conflict-ridden regions, which also highlighted elevated rates of anxiety problems among them.[131]

Furthermore, it is worth noting that various studies have suggested the existence of cultural influences on how anxiety and trauma-related disorders manifest in individuals. These cultural determinants may result in distinct patterns of expression and presentation of such disorders. In essence, these findings underscore the importance of considering cultural factors when examining and addressing anxiety and trauma-related concerns in different populations.[132] This insight is particularly valuable in the field of academic psychology as it helps us understand the nuances of psychological distress in diverse cultural contexts.

Um Fadi recounted the fear and anxiety a wife, mother, and homemaker in Gaza felt every day during the unpredictable Israeli attacks, as she tried to keep her children safe and keep her family together:

> As I was leaving the house, my son told me, let's go this way. I replied, No, let's go this way. He told me, No, let's take this route. I replied, No, this street is closer. Now, it was in the late afternoon, and no one was on the street walking but myself, my son, and my little daughter.
>
> The street my son wanted to take got bombed. I told my son, You see, if we had gone your way, we would have been killed.

---

[131] Thabet & Vostanis, 2002.

[132] Baker & Shalhoub-Kevorkian, 1999; Berman, 2001; Goldstein et al., 1997; Sagi-Schwartz, 2008; Smith et al., 2002; Thabet & Vostanis, 1999.

All Palestinian mothers and fathers had to live daily with the reality that, if their children so much as left the house, they might never return. Yet if they stayed at home, they might have been bombed to death. This kind of prison was intolerable and has led to the mental anguish and symptoms of deeper anxiety that should not be left untreated, as Um Fadi recalled:

The first day and a second day passed, and my son was still not back home. I started to fast with no food or drink. I kept waiting for my son. I turned on the television and I saw a young man killed that looked exactly like my son. I broke down and I started crying. I am in the Zaitona area, an isolated place.

I told my husband; I want to go out. He asked me, where are you going to go to? Are you crazy?! He continued, if it was our son that was killed on the television, we will be informed anyway, and we will take care of it then. My daughters then came and sat with me, and we all started crying.

I told my son, give me your cell phone to call your brother. I phoned, but in the beginning, the call would not go through, until finally it did. My son answered, yes, mother? He then told me that he was on the way home.

I told him, don't let me catch you lying to me about your whereabouts again. What were you thinking? Come home right now—I need you.

He came, and as he entered the door of our house, the house in Shuja'iyya, where he had come from, was hit by an Israeli bomb. It is hard to believe, but that is exactly what happened.

Um Fadi, as with most mothers, felt uncontrollable anxiety about her sons' whereabouts and worried constantly:

We then bought what we needed and went home. When the time to break the fast came, I asked my middle son, 'Where is your brother? We need to be together in ten minutes in order to break the fast.'

However, when an Israeli missile hit, I went out with my children to help the victims. I said, 'Where is your brother?' He replied, 'He will come in a bit.'

Now it's about Magrib time (sunset), with no time left before breaking our fast. I am used to eating with all my children with my husband present, but my oldest child is not home, so I am in grave doubt! I asked again, 'Where is your brother?' He said, 'Mother, he called and told me that he is coming in a bit.' He was not telling the truth.

My son told me, 'Mother, come and eat.' I replied, 'I'll not eat until your brother shows up—where is your brother?' Then, my middle son ate and said, 'Come, I need to tell you something.' I replied, 'What is going on?' He said, 'My brother went out to fight against the invasion and asks that you forgive him if he gets killed.'

Another mother, Asmaa, cannot get the images of death and destruction out of her mind:

Even now, I keep screaming and crying when I remember the time when the Israelis bombed the house, burned it down, and my children. When I remember how me and my daughter fled running without a headscarf and not covered. If people had not put scarves on my head, I mean, the situation was devastating. What we witnessed was tremendously difficult.

Even now, I imagine Israeli war airplanes shelling us with rockets. I start screaming. I was at my parents' house. My family tells me everything is fine and there is nothing wrong. I stayed suffering for two months.

The more I sleep the better I feel, but I still have an anger issue. I cannot tolerate or bear anything. Recently, I was admitted to intensive care at the hospital. I was shivering and I couldn't speak.

Every time Asmaa remembers her family's bombing and death, she experiences a panic attack and starts shivering. When she was admitted to the hospital, she froze and could not speak.

Um Hani's life has also totally changed. I asked her, "On a personal level, was your stability completely destroyed?"

"Yes, that's right," she responded,

> I used to be happy, with my husband and children, and now we're homeless. Now, we are unable to bring money as I go to Gaza with my daughter Nada on foot. We don't have money to go by transportation, and I go back to my house during the hot weather at 1 or 2 pm. I reach my house unable to stand on my legs and suffering from a headache. I speak with you now, and my head is boiling.

> Whenever I remember the past, I become unable to breathe and get nervous. When someone talks to me, I fight with him/her, and I get nervous. I think of how we used to be and how we are now. We are in the street. If I want to go anywhere, I think a lot the whole way. There is nothing that I can do. We used to be happy, and we bought the land here. People told us that it's a safe area, but when the war happened, we were very terrified. When they shell, I became unable to stand on my legs. I prepare myself and my daughters to leave the area. Once I heard the boys saying that the Israelis are at a certain point; therefore, I told my daughter to leave everything and escape.

"What made you nervous?" I asked. "Was it the 2014 war, and the situation you've lived in during the war?"

Um Hani replied, "I am still nervous as at any moment a war might happen. They might shell and make an invasion."

Dr. Kamal Qadih, psychologist at Al-Ghad Al-Mashreq Association, offered a doctor's overview of what is happening to the behavioral patterns of Palestinian children, and how the constant presence of war has caused a built-in anxiety that serves as an emergency alarm that an Israeli attack may be coming:

When they are in the border areas, suddenly Israeli tanks start firing in all directions. Imagine children when they hear the whirring of bullets and the whine of the tanks shelling. Memories of the war and its aggression comes back to the children's minds. When this happens, the children block it from consciousness, because they cannot bear to see and hear tank attacks yet again, for fear of losing their lives. As a result, many children either flee or hide behind the trees and in the hills and ponds and farms.

These overwhelming situations are very scary and frightening. Children will look for anything to hide behind to find security and protection. They believe that a hill or sand block will protect them from the shooting and the tanks. The Israeli attacks don't differentiate between children and the elderly, nor do they care that children are playing and the long-term impact on them will be catastrophic. The children in the Khuza'a area by the Palestinian-Israeli border are continually exposed to and bear this trauma.

Our child clients between the ages of 8-15 years are still in need of psychological care, psychological service, and psychological treatment. One of the main psychological problems children suffer from is their fear of darkness. When the night comes, children are terrified. They run to hide under the bed or in the corners of the house. Also, they run to their mothers' laps. This is a real psychological problem that the child cannot leave his/her parents even at the age of 13-15 years old, thinking that he/she needs his/her mother's lap, believing that it will protect him/her from the terrifying and frightening unknown future.

Gaza Strip suffers from a real problem, namely power outages. Therefore, most of our nights are dark nights, and even the very simple solutions of lighting, such as a candle, caused very large tragedies where children burned in their homes.

They were looking for safety and warmth in the darkness, but the fire from candles burned many of our children, and this was a tragedy and a terrifying experience for all our children. When they see the candle lit in their homes, their immediate expectation is that the candle will burn them as they sleep, and as a result, it is hard for them to fall asleep.

Imagine the feelings of terror, fear, and isolation flying drones create. When they hear the sound of the drones many children directly escape to dark rooms and sleep or hide under tables. When we see a terrified child escaping into the dark, we conceptualize this as regressing to the uterus before birth, where darkness provides the needed feelings of safety and security.

Imagine our children growing up in fear, with shaky personalities, developing into adults who are so fragile that they become captive to the chaos surrounding them all of the time.

Depression

Clinical depression, as defined by the Diagnostic and Statistical Manual of Mental Disorders, Fifth Edition (DSM-5), is characterized by the presence of five or more specific depressive symptoms persisting over a two-week period. These symptoms encompass a range of emotional, cognitive, and physiological manifestations, which collectively contribute to the diagnostic criteria for this mental health condition. These symptoms include:

   a) **Persistent Sadness and Emptiness:** Persons experiencing clinical depression often endure a prolonged sense of profound sadness and emptiness. This emotional state is marked by an overwhelming feeling of inner desolation.
   b) **Frequent Tearfulness or Crying:** Tearfulness and frequent episodes of crying are common in those with clinical depression, reflecting heightened emotional distress and vulnerability.
   c) **Appetite Changes:** Persons with clinical depression may exhibit significant fluctuations in appetite, characterized by either a notable increase or decrease in food consumption on a daily basis.
   d) **Weight Fluctuations:** These shifts in appetite frequently result in consequential changes in body weight, with some persons experiencing

unexplained weight loss, while others may gain weight during depressive episodes.

e) Sleep Disturbances: Sleep patterns are often disrupted in clinical depression. People may either experience excessive sleeping (hypersomnia) or struggle with insomnia, manifesting as difficulty falling asleep or staying asleep.

f) Psychomotor Changes: Clinical depression can influence psychomotor behavior, leading to either increased agitation or a noticeable slowing of movements. This can affect speech patterns, resulting in slowed and subdued communication.

g) Fatigue and Loss of Energy: A pervasive sense of fatigue, accompanied by a persistent loss of energy, is a hallmark of clinical depression. This exhaustion often lingers throughout the day.

h) Feelings of Guilt and Worthlessness: Persons grappling with clinical depression frequently endure feelings of inappropriate guilt and worthlessness. They may excessively dwell on past mistakes or perceived inadequacies.

i) Cognitive Impairments: Cognitive functioning is notably impaired in clinical depression, with affected persons reporting difficulties concentrating, thinking clearly, or making decisions. This may include memory complaints and heightened distractibility.

j) Recurring Thoughts of Death: A distinctive and alarming feature of clinical depression is the presence of recurring thoughts of death. These thoughts extend beyond mere fear of dying and may encompass thoughts of self-harm or suicide.

k) Loss of Interest and Pleasure: Clinical depression often leads to a diminished capacity to derive pleasure from previously enjoyed activities, such as hobbies, sports, or social interactions. This pervasive loss of interest is a prominent symptom.

It's important to note that these symptoms significantly interfere with an individual's daily functioning, social relationships, and overall quality of life. Furthermore, the cognitive impairments associated with clinical depression can lead to marked difficulties in academic and occupational settings. Diagnostic criteria for clinical depression serve as the foundation for assessing and understanding this debilitating mental health condition. The comprehensive evaluation of these symptoms, their duration, and their impact on a person's life are essential for accurate diagnosis and effective intervention in the field of clinical psychology.

As mentioned above, depression is experienced as a loss of interest and energy in things the individual usually enjoys doing (working, going out, or spending time with family and friends). Muntaser Bakr, 14 years old from Gaza City, used to love going to the beach and spend time there but he stopped, his mother reported: "The first time he went back to the beach after the tragedy, he spent a long time looking at the sea and then started crying. He doesn't go back anymore," she added.[133]

As described above, clinical depression is characterized by the persistent experience of five or more of the following depressive symptoms: a pervasive sense of impending doom, disrupted sleep patterns, social withdrawal, profound emotional isolation, diminished attention span, profound despair stemming from witnessing life's grim reality, and a debilitating inability to engage in daily activities due to overwhelming fear of impending events.[134] The Palestinian population, specifically children, has exhibited a prevalence of depressive disorders. This condition is marked by a profound sense of existential dread, heightened anticipation of future events, sleep disturbances, a proclivity towards isolation, reduced attentional capacity, and a deep-seated apprehension rooted in the bleak and challenging realities of life, which hinders autonomous functioning.[135]

The Middle East and North Africa (MENA) region, particularly Palestine, has alarmingly high rates of depression and anxiety disorders. According to estimates, more than 40% of Palestinians grapple with clinical depression, marking the highest prevalence globally. This alarming statistic underscores the urgent need for comprehensive mental health initiatives and interventions to alleviate the suffering of the Palestinian population

---

[133] Al-Haddad, 2017, "Muntaser Bakr," para. 6.

[134] *DSM-5*, American Psychiatric Association, 2013.

[135] Khamis, 2018.

and enhance their psychological well-being.[136] An example is Asmaa, who has changed completely because of what happened to her during the war: "I cannot tolerate or bear anything anymore. If my daughter or my son got sad, I can't bear seeing that. I start shivering. A short while ago my daughter had an argument with her husband. I was admitted to intensive care in the hospital."

Um Hani and her family deal with the aftermath of the war every day. "In the 2014 war," I said, "you lost your house and security, and until now you still suffer from the same thing. Do you believe that those effects will continue into the future?

"Yes, I do," she replied. "My son, who used to work and bring money for us, was injured in his fingers and has 16 stitches. Yesterday, my second son suffered an injury while he was working, and his vein was nearly cut. We only say thanks be to Allah, and yes, my life will change in the future."

Um Fadi, like many others, fell into depression over the state of her life and the lives of her children. I began this conversation by saying, "During the war of 2014, you lost your home, got displaced, and were sent to a shelter. After that, you returned home but you couldn't stay in it. After the truce, how did you feel?"

"I felt like I am finished, done, everything is gone."

"Some women told me they felt sad and had a nervous breakdown," I said.

Um Fadi replied: "Until now, when I enter my apartment, I feel depressed and sad. Until

now I feel life is impossible and lived in shock. Remembering my home, I cry so hard I choke. I feel like fighting with my kids all of the time. Then my girls ask me to please forget the tragedy we have gone through. I tell them I cannot forget, it's impossible to forget.

"I used to live in a house made of bricks, now I am living in a broken-down house covered with a metal roof. I pray to the Lord to have a home again where there are no mice, cockroaches, and flies. I hope my daughters can feel free in their home. Ugh, if you could see their room.

---

[136] Elbedour, Onwuegbuzie, Ghannam, Whitcome, & Hein, 2007.

God willing you will come and see how it looks."

I asked, "When you experience depression, anxiety, or a nervous breakdown do you seek help from a friend, relative or the mental health clinic, so that you can talk to them about your condition?"

"I talked to a psychologist," she said. "I told him about the pain I have in my heart, what can I do with that?"

Um Fadi's poignant question on how to heal her heart is one that every Palestinian is asking. The vital need to nourish their hearts is what has led to increased emphasis on providing mental health services to these walking wounded. Mental health services, as evidenced in the conversation below, contribute greatly to emotional health, as well.

As a follow-up on the therapy I knew she participated in, I asked Um Fadi, "How do you use drawing to release your feelings, as you were taught at the club?"

> When I first came, and we started the group therapy they asked me to draw. I was tired and exhausted, and I was not happy the first time. But after they taught us breathing, I started to feel comfortable. Honestly, now I am so happy that I joined the group therapy that I even bring my daughters. It's been two years since I started attending the group therapy sessions in Juhor ad-Dik.

> They taught us how to care for our health, how to deal with our children, how to deal with my daughter when she gets her period, how to deal with my son, how to control my anger. Thank the Lord they taught us so many things.

Wa'd, as a girl, had a hard time adjusting to postwar circumstances:

> The war was horrifying and terrible on every level. I found myself psychologically trapped and afraid. I found myself with no safe place, not even my own home. Psychologically I am tired of the word "war," we are children and there is no place safe for us. I am getting tired just hearing the word "war."

I am living in a place where I do not have safety and no comfort. Suddenly, I am living in a strange place, I do not know what to do. All my life suddenly crumbled to ashes, all I am hearing is this person died, this person is alive. Psychologically you are destroyed. I only hear the news of so-and-so died, suddenly his life is over, but once the war ended, half of the city is gone and left in ruins by the Israeli bombardment.

Hyperactivity

Hyperactivity, as defined by the American Psychiatric Association, is characterized by a persistent pattern of inattention and/or hyperactivity-impulsivity that surpasses what is typically observed in individuals at a comparable level of development.[137] Those affected by hyperactivity often experience heightened levels of anxiety and depression due to their condition and the reactions of those around them. Additionally, individuals with hyperactivity may encounter various challenges stemming from their inability to maintain stillness or focus. For instance, in children, hyperactivity may lead to academic difficulties, accidents, and injuries. Common characteristics of hyperactivity include aggressive behavior, easy distractibility, constant movement, and impulsive actions.

One of the primary disorders associated with hyperactivity is Attention Deficit Hyperactivity Disorder (ADHD). ADHD is a neurodevelopmental syndrome characterized by impulsivity, hyperactivity, and inattention.[138] Although typically diagnosed in childhood, some individuals continue to experience ADHD symptoms into adulthood. Hyperactivity symptoms in children can manifest as difficulties concentrating in school, impulsivity (e.g., speaking out of turn, excessive activity), and disruptive behavior towards peers. These challenges may contribute to feelings of anxiety and depression in affected children.

It is important to recognize that hyperactivity often serves as a symptom of an underlying cause, which can encompass both medical

---

[137] APA, 2013.
[138] APA, 2013.

and mental health conditions. Among the most prevalent contributing factors are hyperthyroidism, which involves an excessive production of thyroid hormones, as well as various brain and nervous system disorders. Additionally, psychological disorders can contribute to the manifestation of hyperactivity symptoms. For example, research has indicated a significant relationship between traumatic brain injuries (TBI) and changes in ADHD symptomatology. A study involving 50 children aged 6 to 14 years hospitalized after TBI revealed that the severity of injury was closely linked to alterations in ADHD symptom presentation within the first two years post-injury.[139] Notably, some participants in this study experienced TBI due to the 2014 Israeli war, which played a substantial role in the elevated prevalence of hyperactivity disorder in this population.[140] These findings are supported by other research studies of traumatic brain injury and hyperactivity disorder.[141] In summary, hyperactivity is characterized by a persistent pattern of heightened activity and impulsivity that exceeds typical developmental expectations. This condition, often associated with ADHD, can lead to various challenges in individuals, particularly children, including academic difficulties, accidents, and emotional distress. Furthermore, hyperactivity may serve as a symptom of underlying medical, neurological, or psychological conditions, emphasizing the need for comprehensive assessment and intervention strategies. Dr. Kamal Qadih discussed hyperactivity during our interview:

> Frightening disorders such as hyperactivity are producing abnormal individuals. These abnormal Palestinians have experienced Israeli aggression repeatedly visited upon them. As a result of their fear of Israeli aggression, they have become so aggressive they threaten or harm citizens of our own society and they pose a threat of harm to themselves.

---

[139] Gerring, Brady, Chen, Vasa, Grados, Bandeen-Roche, & Bryan, 1998.

[140] Max et al., 1998.

[141] Cf. Cruickshank, 1961; Konrad, Gauggel, Manz, & Schöll, 2000.

Dr. Qadih has seen a dangerous shift in the postwar behavior of his people:

> In addition to the fear of Israeli aggression, citizens of our own society have become so aggressive that they pose a threat of harm to themselves or others. Frightening disorders such as insomnia, nail biting, isolation, introversion, hyperactivity, and withdrawal, all exist on a very large scale, and are resulting in the development of abnormal individuals. These abnormal Palestinian individuals would otherwise be mature and healthy citizens if not for the Israeli aggression that has been repeatedly visited upon them.

Muntaser Bakr, age 14, was bombed by the Israelis with other young relatives and friends while playing football on the beach and saw the death of his brother during that bombing. His mother bemoans the changes in her son:

> Since the tragedy, he went back to school once. He fought with one of his classmates and hit him with a chair. He no longer attends school. Muntaser suffers from seizures 3-4 times a week. It happens unexpectedly. He starts screaming and then experiences a spasm, loses consciousness, his eyes roll back, and he starts clenching his jaw. He does not calm down until we take him to a hospital to get an injection.

Social withdrawal

Social withdrawal is described by the American Psychiatric Association as "a persistent fear of one or more social or performance situations in which the person is exposed to unfamiliar people or to possible scrutiny by others. The individual fears that he or she will act in a way (or show anxiety symptoms) that will be embarrassing and humiliating."[142] Social withdrawal

---

[142] APA, 2013, p. 202.

is a notable behavioral manifestation characterized by individuals actively seeking to avoid both social interactions and activities that they would typically find enjoyable.

In certain cases, this inclination towards social withdrawal can escalate into a condition referred to as social isolation, where individuals exhibit a preference for solitude even to the extent of distancing themselves from close family and friends. This inclination to be alone often arises from a perception that social engagement is either physically or emotionally draining, or simply distressing. Those afflicted by this disorder may encounter impediments in engaging in their usual activities and managing their daily lives. Consequently, the ramifications of this condition can encompass feelings of loneliness, interpersonal difficulties, disrupted sleep patterns, and even the development of alcohol-related problems. If social withdrawal or isolation remains unaddressed, it may ultimately contribute to, or coincide with, the onset of depression.

The absence of social interactions in a child's life can stem from various factors, such as social anxiety or a preference for solitude. Children who tend to withdraw socially are vulnerable to a range of negative outcomes in their emotional and social development. These consequences encompass emotional challenges, including anxiety, depression, internalizing issues, low self-esteem, feelings of helplessness, and a lack of self-confidence. Socially withdrawn children often avoid participating in social activities with their peers, which can lead to difficulties in their peer relationships. These challenges may manifest as poor-quality friendships, rejection, victimization, and difficulties in effectively interacting with others. Furthermore, socially withdrawn children may encounter academic and school-related difficulties, which may involve strained relationships with teachers, academic struggles, avoidance of school, and a general sense of distrust towards others.[143] It is essential to note that socially withdrawn children can face even more significant problems if they lose their sense of security or become victims of aggression, conflict, or physical injuries, such as limb loss or visual impairment.

---

[143] Rubin, Coplan, & Bowker, 2009.

War has had a profound and enduring impact on the emotional and psychological well-being of children across generations. Numerous studies and research findings have documented the extensive and long-lasting consequences of exposure to war-related trauma on children's mental health. Studies have shown that one out of three children who live in war zones could develop some form of lower psychosocial functioning level during their lifetime due to the volatile and violent environment they lived in.[144] Exposure to violence, loss of loved ones, displacement, and disrupted access to education and healthcare can contribute to long-lasting psychological and emotional scars in children. [145]

This impact is not limited to the immediate generation but often extends to subsequent generations, creating a cycle of trauma and psychological distress. Research has consistently demonstrated that children growing up in war zones experience a wide range of emotional and psychological challenges that persist throughout their lives.

One of the seminal studies on the long-term effects of war on children was conducted by Rachel Yehuda and her colleagues, who examined the intergenerational transmission of trauma in Holocaust survivors and their offspring. They found that children of Holocaust survivors exhibited higher rates of post-traumatic stress disorder (PTSD), depression, and anxiety compared to individuals without a family history of trauma. [146]

Another noteworthy study conducted by Theresa S. Betancourt and her team examined the psychosocial impact of war on children in Sierra Leone, a country that experienced a brutal civil war. Their research revealed that children exposed to the violence and trauma of war were at increased risk of developing emotional and behavioral problems, including depression, anxiety, and conduct disorders. [147]

Furthermore, the effects of war can extend beyond a single generation. Research by Catrin Rees and colleagues in Northern Uganda highlighted

---

[144] The Dyregrov, Gjestad, and Raundalen, 2002.

[145] UNICEF, 2020.

[146] The Dyregrov, Yehuda, R., Halligan, & Grossman, 2001.

[147] Betancourt, Borisova, Williams, Meyers-Ohki, Rubin-Smith, Annan, J., ... & Kohrt, 2010.

how the experiences of war can be transmitted to subsequent generations. They found that the offspring of individuals who had experienced conflict-related trauma were more likely to exhibit symptoms of PTSD, suggesting an intergenerational transfer of trauma.[148]

According to Save the Children, Palestinian children face numerous barriers to social engagement due to the ongoing conflict. These barriers include restricted movement caused by Israeli checkpoints and the separation barrier, which limit access to educational and recreational facilities. Furthermore, frequent military incursions into Palestinian territories disrupt daily life and pose a constant threat to children's safety, discouraging them from participating in social activities.[149] A study by psychologists Qouta, Punamäki and El Sarraj found that the continued exposure to traumatic events, including the loss of family members and friends, has a profound emotional impact on Palestinian children. A study published in the Journal of Traumatic Stress (Qouta et al., 2008) found that children in the Gaza Strip displayed high levels of emotional distress and social withdrawal as a result of their experiences during the conflict. These emotional and psychological consequences can hinder children's ability to form and maintain social relationships.[150] The United Nations Children's Fund (UNICEF) has documented the impact of the conflict on Palestinian children, highlighting the significant disruptions to their daily lives. In its reports, UNICEF has pointed out that many children in Gaza and the West Bank are forced to stay indoors, unable to play or socialize with their peers at playgrounds, parks, or other public spaces, for fear of violence erupting at any moment.[151]

According to a report by Human Rights Watch (HRW), the Israeli military's practices, such as demolishing schools and detaining students, have disrupted the educational process for Palestinian children, contributing to their social isolation (HRW, 2019). The lack of access

---

[148] Rees, Keane, & Shea, 2011.

[149] Save the Children, 2019.

[150] Qouta, Punamäki, & El Sarraj, 2008.

[151] Children in the State of Palestine, n.d.

to quality education further exacerbates feelings of hopelessness and withdrawal. [152] The results of this study showed that due to the Israeli war and aggression, social withdrawal is evident among Palestinian children. The fact that Palestinian children are no longer able to live a normal life, nor able to practice their daily activities, such as playing at the playground or going for a swim at the beautiful Mediterranean Sea is a heartbreaking consequence of the Israeli violence and insecurity that has persisted for decades. Instead, they are forced to withdraw from daily activities and hide in their homes to protect their lives due to their fear of bombing, shelling, or a stray bullet.

Asmaa is an example of someone who exhibits social withdrawal. She cannot forget what happened, and it has caused her to turn inward and not communicate:

> In the case of understanding other people, it has become normal to not be able to tolerate anyone. When someone criticizes me, I become sensitive. When my husband criticizes me, I get mad, and I can't stand my kids. I hit them, and I insult them. I can't stand anyone in the house; I can't stand myself. I'm living on painkillers.

The HRW findings are indicative of the significant psychological toll that war and conflict can have on children in regions like the Gaza Strip. These findings are supported by various studies conducted by researchers in the field of child psychology and trauma. One such study, involving 56 war-exposed Palestinian children in the Gaza Strip, revealed alarming statistics. Approximately 37.8% of these children were diagnosed with PTSD. This diagnosis sheds light on the severity of the psychological impact of conflict on these children. Notably, the children in this study exhibited a range of posttraumatic symptoms, and their psychological distress manifested in ways that are deeply concerning. One particularly disturbing aspect was the substantial developmental regression observed in these children. This regression suggests that the trauma they experienced

---

[152] HRW, 2019.

had a profound and lasting impact on their emotional and cognitive development. Among the prevalent symptoms observed in more than 60% of the diagnosed children was social withdrawal.[153] This symptom is indicative of the profound isolation and emotional turmoil these children were experiencing as a result of their exposure to war and conflict. The withdrawal from social interactions can have long-lasting consequences on their ability to form healthy relationships and engage with their communities. Furthermore, a study conducted in 2008 focused on the developmental outcomes of Palestinian children living in Gaza who had lost their homes due to conflict. This study highlighted that a staggering 60% of these children suffered from intrusive memories, re-experiencing trauma, social withdrawal symptoms, and night terrors.[154] These symptoms are characteristic of the psychological distress and fear that pervades the lives of children living in conflict zones.

Wa'd was certain that death awaited her – her experience illustrates the overwhelming fear and uncertainty that these children endure on a daily basis, further exacerbating their psychological trauma. She talked about her experience:

> The situation in the schools (shelters) was very bad and crowded, and diseases were spread. People were on the top of each other, more than fifty people, mixed boys, girls, and families. The place was not comfortable. I had to wear my headscarf and my full garment 24 hours. I got Meningitis from the fear and mixing with other people. Psychologically, I was tired from being displaced from my home, and my town. In addition, the schools were a public place with so many people in the same room lumped together.
>
> After that I went to the hospital and stayed two weeks without treatment. I only slept, living on an IV. When I was released from the hospital, I was a little bit better and I returned to the school. Because of the cold water I was bathing with, my hair

---

[153] Feldman and Vengrober, 2011.

[154] Qouta, Punamäki, and El Sarraj, 2008.

suddenly started falling out from the front and the back, and it became very rough.

Psychologically, I wanted to stay away from people and isolate myself, waiting for death. We were just waiting for death; you hear that so-and-so died, then you say to yourself our turn is coming. This is how we felt, this person is gone and our turn is coming.

I sat alone 24 hours. I did not like anyone's company. I concluded that this is the best for me and I got used to it. It was almost an entire year that I sat alone. I am used to sitting by myself and not talking to anyone.

"Have you tried to seek help? A psychologist?" I asked her. "I went," she said, "but I didn't speak because I got tired as soon as I remembered the memories of the war, I get tired, that's all." Then she was silent.

Aggression

Numerous studies have highlighted how the atmosphere of war, hostility, military violence, aggression, and exposure to traumatic events can compromise the healthy emotional development of children, increase their risk for aggressive behavior, and predict negative outcomes in child development.

Empirical evidence supporting the link between violent experiences and aggressive behavior primarily stems from research conducted in American inner cities where children have been exposed to a range of traumatic events such as armed robberies, violent detentions, shootings, and killings. The findings consistently reveal a higher prevalence of general aggression and emotional expression disorders in children who have witnessed such violence compared to children not exposed to such experiences. These studies underscore the negative impact of exposure to violence on children's emotional well-being and their propensity to engage in aggressive behaviors. [155] These observations align with social

---

[155] Attanayake, McKay, Joffres, Singh, Burkle, & Mills, 2009.

learning models of aggression, which propose that children learn violent behaviors by modeling and imitating those around them, especially in crime-intensive environments. Consequently, children growing up in such environments are at an increased risk of exhibiting aggressive tendencies as they imitate the violent behaviors they witness. [156]

The global context also provides evidence of the adverse effects of war and aggression on children's emotional development. For instance, during the 1970s in Cambodia, the 1980s in Mozambique and Angola, and in regions with protracted conflicts such as Palestine and Northern Ireland, children have been repeatedly exposed to the horrors of war and military violence. In these contexts, it has been observed that children who experience firsthand war and aggression often develop aggressive behaviors as a result.[157] One illustrative study highlights the impact of conflict on Palestinian children living in the Gaza Strip. During periods of Israeli-imposed curfew and the Palestinian uprising in 1987, approximately 66% of Palestinian children were found to engage in fights with each other, and 38% developed aggressive behavior. These figures underscore how exposure to conflict and aggression can lead to a significant rise in aggressive behaviors among children in conflict zones.[158] Additionally, research has shown a heightened risk of posttraumatic symptoms among children exposed to severe war trauma during their early years. For instance, Croatian adolescents who experienced traumatic events during their preschool age exhibited a higher level of aggressive behavior compared to children who were less exposed to such trauma.[159]

The impact of exposure to military violence on the behavior of Palestinian children has been a subject of significant research and concern. One study conducted on this topic found that Palestinian children who were exposed to severe military violence, which included witnessing killings, losses, and injuries, exhibited increased levels of aggressive and

[156] Smith, Cowie, Olafsson, & Liefooghe, 2002.

[157] Margolin, & Gordis, 2000.

[158] Qouta, Punamäki, & El Sarraj, 2008.

[159] Deković, & Meeus, 1997.

antisocial behavior.[160] This particular study aimed to investigate the relationship between the exposure to different forms of military violence (direct victimization and witnessing) and the manifestation of various forms of aggression (reactive, proactive, and aggression enjoyment) among Palestinian children. The findings from this research revealed a significant association between children's exposure to severe military violence and their subsequent aggressive and antisocial behaviors. These behaviors were reported both by the children themselves and by their parents. Palestinian children exhibited aggression towards both themselves and their peers, and this behavior was attributed to their daily exposure to Israeli military violence in the Gaza Strip.[161] Furthermore, these findings were substantiated through interviews conducted with psychologists and social workers affiliated with the Gaza Community Mental Health Programme (GCMHP), who observed similar patterns of aggressive and antisocial behavior among Palestinian children as a result of their exposure to military violence. These professionals' accounts provided additional validation of the study's results, highlighting the profound impacts of ongoing military aggression on the psychological well-being and behavior of Palestinian children in the region. In addition, these results were confirmed by other studies.[162] A research conducted by Qouta and colleagues (2003) is consistent with other studies that have explored the impact of Israeli military aggression on Palestinian children. For instance, another study found that an overwhelming 95% of Palestinian children aged 7 to 12 years in their sample had been exposed to Israeli military aggression, further emphasizing the widespread nature of this exposure and its potential influence on children's behavior.[163] Dr. Kamal Qadih sees a troubling growth of psychologically impaired people being conditioned by violence to be aggressive, and who do not have sufficient resources to address the problems:

[160] Qouta, Punamäki, Miller, & El Sarraj, 2008.

[161] Qouta, Punamäki, Miller, and El Sarraj, 2008.

[162] Barber, 1999; Dimitry, 2012; Qouta et al., 2003; Qouta, Punamäki, Miller, & El Sarraj, 2008.

[163] Hein et al., 1993.

Imagine a young and innocent child becoming an aggressive person as a direct result of the various forms of aggression he witnessed in his life, such as the killing, bombing, injuries, and destruction of his home. Such children cannot help but become aggressive, it is the way nature is preparing them to fight the battles of the next generation. Without alternative psychological models, children learn aggression by modeling what they know and have been exposed to, thus repeating a vicious cycle.

For our children to become aggressive is not acceptable. We want our children to be peaceful, compassionate, and loving. This requires us to gather all available resources and produce sustained effort, to give the children the psychological, economic, and societal support they need to have dignified personal and social lives.

Children in conflict zones often develop aggressive behaviors as a consequence of the pervasive violence and aggression directed towards them and their families, creating a distressing cycle of violence begetting more violence. Furthermore, societal norms and expectations play a crucial role in shaping which emotions are accepted and appreciated among these children. In contexts of war and military violence, expressions of aggression, anger, and boldness towards the perceived enemy are often encouraged and considered virtuous by their families and communities. Conversely, feelings of helplessness, fear, and compassion toward the enemy may be stigmatized and suppressed. These socially promoted emotions not only serve as coping mechanisms but also serve to dull the awareness of extreme physical and emotional pain that children may be experiencing. However, research suggests that traumatized children who habitually suppress their emotions may display uncontrollable and impulsive behavior as a result. [164]Impulsiveness, in this context, may manifest as a tendency to translate intense feelings and tensions into direct action without undergoing emotional processing or cognitive evaluation. Some studies have suggested that parents may be more tolerant of violence

---

[164] Dalgleish et al., 2003.

initiated in self-defense, as it aligns with their understanding of their children's engagement in political activities However, they are deeply concerned about the detrimental effects of violence on their children's psychological development, including increased aggression and constrained future prospects.[165] In their daily lives, Palestinian children face numerous situations and incidents during times of war that contribute to their frustration. Frustration, in this context, arises from their inability to attain their desires or the loss of cherished possessions and security (Davis, 20BB). These children endure a continuous stream of daily frustrations that accumulate over years due to the occupation and recurring conflicts, which erode their sense of security and trust in their environment. Witnessing Israeli attacks on authority figures and protectors further amplifies their frustrations.

During wartime, Israeli forces often engage in actions such as bombing homes, causing harm to family members, and destroying essential items like food, clothing, toys, and books. These actions evoke strong feelings of anger and resentment among Palestinian children and fuel motives for revenge and hatred. This internalized anger becomes a potent force that stimulates a spirit of violence and resistance as children perceive a constant threat to their lives. Through this research I want to clarify that the lives of Palestinian children are marked by a multitude of frustrations stemming from the political situation and the years of conflict they have endured. These frustrations, coupled with the successive traumas inflicted by Israeli actions, have accumulated throughout their psychosocial development stages, leading to the normalization of violence as a means of defending their needs and homes. This normalization manifests in various ways, including children participating in games that simulate war and violence, engaging in play with toy guns, displaying aggression towards peers and others' property, self-harming behaviors, and a tendency to reject advice and guidance without fully comprehending the consequences of their actions.

---

[165] Kira et al., 2013.

Earlier research findings support this narrative, with studies indicating that 66% of Palestinian children fought with each other more during the times when Israeli occupation imposed a curfew on them than when there was no curfew, and 38% developed aggressive behavior.[166] Additionally, traumatic events have been associated with both direct and indirect aggression, affecting not only peer relations but also creating conflicts within sibling relationships. A study of 240 Palestinian children between the ages of 11 and 13 showed that traumatic events were associated with both direct and indirect aggression. The results of the study also showed that "traumatic events can complicate social relations: peer relations are better and sibling relations conflicting among children with severe trauma."[167] Furthermore, a study of 1,500 Middle Eastern children and their parents, Palestinians, and Israeli Jews, showed that ethno-political violence in the Middle East has been linked to increased aggression and school violence among Palestinian and Israeli children.[168]

Ultimately, the cycle of Israeli aggression towards Palestinian children has resulted in aggression being directed inward, causing these children to exhibit aggressive behaviors towards their peers and even their own family members. The trauma experienced during the war influenced how children relate to their peers, with some children exhibiting aggressive behaviors, and others becoming withdrawn or anxious.

Asmaa learned to understand violent reactions to her children's behavior. One of her children, who experienced the 2014 war and witnessed the death of family members, dealt with his trauma by fighting with his peers. On many occasions, Asmaa's child has been aggressive towards children in the neighborhood. Asmaa had to bear the consequences of her child's behavior. On one occasion, her child fought with her best friend's son, which aggravated her best friend. Asmaa expressed her feelings about the incident in our interview:

[166] Qouta and El Sarraj, 1992.
[167] Qouta, Punamäki, & El Sarraj, 2008, p. 313.
[168] Boxer et al., 2013.

One thing that made me disappointed is that my best friend started shouting and cursing me and my children for a tiny mistake. In the morning, she came and ruined my day because my little boy made a little mistake. She came shouting, screaming and wanting to hit the boy. I told her if he gives you a hard time you can hit him, but please don't start screaming and shouting at me in front of people on the street, I feel saddened by this.

I discussed this interaction with several psychiatrists and psychologists in Gaza. Unfortunately, this is the result of the psychological repression that exists in the people, and this is one of the remnants of the existing war, which a lot of politicians or non-politicians are not aware of. Most people in Gaza suffer from a psychological nervous breakdown, they are expressing their psychological repression with erroneous behavior, including shouting, insulting, humiliating others, and insulting children and women.

Wael worries about his son. I asked him, "Have you noticed any changes in your son's behavior since the injury?"

"From the day of the injury to this day, he is very evil and stubborn and nervous. He always hits his sister and his relatives. Attacking and cursing."

"Does your son sometimes get very scared?"

"Sometimes accompanied by panic attacks," Wael said. "The previous period, he was waking up at night in his sleep, screaming loudly and crying and breaking anything in front of him. Currently, he is so attached to his grandfather that he sleeps next to him, and if he leaves his hand he wakes up from sleep and cries screaming."

Wael's son, Sharif, was quiet, but answered one question. "Sharif, are you afraid when you hear the sound of a reconnaissance plane?"

"Yes," responded Sharif.

"Why?"

Sharif remained silent.

"Wael," I said, "please tell me why Sharif is afraid when he hears the sound of a reconnaissance plane."

"Because Sharif has seen the whole event before his eyes," Wael said. "When we were bombed by the reconnaissance plane, he thought it killed us, and from that moment he was afraid to hear the sound of it in the sky."

Dr. Kamal Qadih sees a disturbing trend of psychologically impaired people unleashing their inner demons, due to lack of attention and insufficient resources to address the problems. I broached the topic of prolonged psychological effects: "We have heard about the death tolls and injuries of the 2014 war; however, we don't hear about the long-term psychological effects on women, men, and especially children. There are deep psychological effects. One of my primary interests is in the psychological impact of the war on children." Dr. Qadih responded:

> The truth is that Palestinians, young or old, continue to hold pain and agony in their psyche. When I completed my Ph.D. in mental health, I focused my studies on the 2003 war and subsequent wars against Palestinians. Nowadays, if I ask a child to talk about their life, their reply will be, my life is all wars. Some children have been through three wars, and the Palestinian people are afraid of a fourth one.

> For example, I found that most school students carry a sharp tool to attack the property of others. Also, they deal with their peers as if they are the ones, rather than the Israelis, who assaulted them during the war and left them in pain and suffering. The children try to relieve their negative emotions in this way by projecting their aggravation and frustration on their friends, or on the property of others.

War exacts a severe toll on the mental well-being of both children and adults, leaving a profound impact on the affected population's way of life. The crisis in Palestine presents a dire situation wherein the mental health of an entire nation is in jeopardy. Over the past decade, multiple research studies have shed light on the alarming prevalence of mental health issues among various segments of the Palestinian populace, including children, adolescents, women, refugees, and prisoners.[169] A comprehensive study conducted during the Second Intifada examined Palestinian perceptions of their living conditions, revealing distressing findings. Among the surveyed parents, 46% reported observing aggressive behavior in their children, while 38% expressed concern over deteriorating academic performance. Bedwetting was reported by 27% of parents, and 39% noted that their children suffered from distressing nightmares. Interestingly, the study noted a higher incidence of aggressive behavior among refugee children (53%) compared to non-refugee children (41%). The study further delved into the factors contributing to these distressing outcomes. Shockingly, 38% of respondents attributed the escalation in aggressive behavior to exposure to shooting incidents, while 34% believed that violence depicted on television played a significant role. Additionally, 7% cited the confinement of children within their homes as a contributing factor, while 11% pointed to the arrest and physical abuse of relatives and neighbors as traumatic experiences influencing the children's mental state. Equally concerning is the finding that a staggering 70% of both refugees and non-refugees reported that they had not received any form of psychological support to address the emotional and psychological challenges faced by their children. This lack of adequate support further exacerbates the mental health crisis, underscoring the urgent need for intervention and resources to address the profound mental health issues stemming from the ongoing conflict in Palestine.[170]

---

[169] Qouta & El Sarraj, 2002.

[170] Mousa & Madi, 2003.

CHAPTER 4:

"Filling a bottomless bucket with water"

The 2014 Israeli conflict in Gaza inflicted profound psychological trauma upon a substantial number of Palestinian children. According to the United Nations, virtually every child residing in Gaza was left in need of psychosocial support, with an alarming estimate of approximately 373,000 children requiring specialized psychological support.[171] This crisis, however, cannot be seen in isolation; it is inexorably intertwined with the enduring impact of Israel's half-century occupation of the West Bank and Gaza, which has heavily impacted the mental well-being of Palestinians. A comprehensive study underscores the intricate web of factors contributing to the deterioration of mental health among young Palestinians. The cumulative burden of environmental stressors, perpetuated through generations of conflict and war, has cast a long shadow over the minds of these children. The findings of this research reveal that a staggering 54% of Palestinian boys and 46.5% of Palestinian girls between the ages of 6 and 12 are anticipated to grapple with emotional and behavioral disorders as a consequence of their circumstances.[172] These studies, alongside the insights offered by this book, delve deep into the nexus between the Israeli conflict of 2014 and its corrosive effects on the mental health of Gaza's young population. The conclusions are unequivocal: the Israeli military campaign had a profoundly detrimental impact on the psychological well-being of Palestinian children, emerging as one of the foremost catalysts behind the pervasive mental and psychological challenges they face.

---

[171] UN, 2014.

[172] Charara et al., 2017.

The extent of violence and aggression unleashed by Israeli forces upon Palestinian children—comprising aerial bombardments, fatalities, the razing of homes and properties, incursions into towns, villages, and refugee camps with tanks and munitions, and the deliberate destruction of vital institutions such as schools, hospitals, and farms—contributed to the fracturing of the psychological resilience of Palestinian children. These findings underscore the stark reality that repeated acts of aggression and warfare have had a profound and lasting impact on the psychological equilibrium of Palestinian children, giving rise to conditions such as post-traumatic stress disorder, anxiety, depression, social withdrawal, and heightened tendencies towards aggression.

Amir Ibrahim Al Reqeb, a child of nine, has suffered grievous injuries, including damage to his skull and fractured bones in his jaw and shrapnel wounds that have punctuated his body, particularly his lungs and eye. As a result, Amir finds himself in a perpetual state of anxiety and vulnerability. Any sudden loud noise, the rumbling of a thunderstorm, or the drone of Israeli warplanes sends him running to his parents. At night, he is tormented by night terrors. His mother describes his nightly ritual: "He clings to his pillow and follows me, placing it upon my lap. If he awakens and finds neither myself nor his father nearby, he is overcome with distress."[173]

Malak Abu Jamous, 9 years old, from Khan Yunis, witnessed the death of her beloved grandfather, a tragedy that unfolded at the hands of Israeli soldiers during the 2014 war on Gaza.

In happier times, Malak had been a vivacious child, spending the majority of her days with her grandfather, Salman. She says, "He was the one who gave me an allowance." When she misses him, Malak looks at a photograph of him and asks, "When will he return?" Ahlam tells her daughter, "No, my dear, he has ascended to heaven." Malak asks her father the same question. He responds with: "Do those who have departed from this world ever return?" Malak responds, "Yes, my grandfather will return." Malak suffers post-traumatic stress, manifested through debilitating

---

[173] Al-Haddad, 2017, "Amir Ibrahim Al Reqeb," para. 8.

symptoms such as recurring headaches, involuntary incontinence, and sudden nervous outbursts. Her mother says that on one occasion, she inexplicably spilled cooking kerosene onto the bathroom floor, offering no explanation for her actions. "At night Malak becomes distressed, yelling "Get away from me!" Ahlam laments that her daughter, who used to be a happy, social girl, has difficulty interacting with anyone now.

Zahia al-Qarra, a psychologist of the Gaza Community Mental Health Programme, said the prolonged war continued to evoke ugly memories, which had once been present in children's imaginations. "The end of the war does not mean the children are safe," she said.[174] Permanent power cuts, continuing Israeli war plane flights, the drones that fly over Gaza all day and night long, and media talk of war have lowered the morale of children. According to al-Qarra, it causes them to be haunted by trauma. Dr. Sami Owaida, a psychiatric consultant for children and adolescents from the GCMHP, explained the symptoms of psychological trauma appearing in children in various ways. "Physically, they can manifest trauma through headaches, pain in the abdomen and joints, as well as delusions, without any real cause." He added:

> Behavioral symptoms will show withdrawn or aggressive behavior, as well as causing feelings of insecurity, anxiety, fear, and pessimism. But instead of thinking of things that are appropriate to their childhood, they begin to fear other possible trauma; cognitively they will appear very bad at school.

Dr. Owaida expressed frustration with the deteriorating mental health situation and explained that he and his staff were limited in helping victims due to the political tensions surrounding Gaza. Nonetheless, they try, he explained:

> All we do is put a bandage on the wound, it is purely a grafting process. There is an Arab saying, filling a bottomless bucket with

---

[174] Al-Haddad, 2017, "Amir Ibrahim Al Reqeb," para. 10.

water. Why? Because the children understand, it means we do what is possible. A child asks a question: Are you able to prevent new aggression and stop the killing of my mother or sister?

Unfortunately, let me tell you, it is useless, but we do what is required! Should we just do nothing? No, we try as much as possible with the means available to do something. But so that the media does not shade public opinion, they must understand that aggression can be repeated at any moment, and the process of restraint must be at the political level.

The subject is purely political and therefore the process of control should come from a political solution to the radical issue, which is to end the occupation.

Dr. Owaida is resigned to doing only what he can, but also hopeful that more will be done, based upon several treatment programs catering to those in need.

All we can do is to cope with the existing situation. To meet the urgent need, for example, there are several treatment centers in the Gaza Strip. There are the governmental and the civil level, the NGOs, which are the best and the most effective. It provides a clinical treatment service, and this is the difference between other institutions that specialize in psycho-social work.

There are different types of psychiatry which we follow in the treatment, and use all the standards used abroad, which are parallel treatment sessions for parents. We focus on parents strongly because they are the source of support and inspiration for children, because if parents are worried and have psychological problems, we cannot treat the child without a treatment reference.

Children's sessions vary, according to the initial diagnosis of the child, because we diagnose children who suffer from psychological trauma and are in a situation where they cannot express feelings. We are working to stimulate them to express through other means, such as writing, drawing, and playing.

Dr. Owaida is focused on whole-family healing, working with parents as well as children. Yet he concedes that ultimately he hopes only to make life tolerable for Palestinians in what he calls this prison of the Gaza Strip:

> There are also new techniques to use in coordination with parents. There are home visits for those who cannot visit us. There are encouraging ways to deal with kindergartens and even schools. There are huge national plans. It is how we work to investigate or explore these situations and guides how we handle these children and take necessary healing actions.

> There are large plans at the internal level to explore these cases and deal with them early. There are huge projects carried out even at the level of the World Health Organization related to the integration of mental health care, even addressing the stigma level of people who feel humiliated by their condition. There are many projects used to deal with these cases, and to at least guarantee the continuation of normal life as much as possible in this great prison where the children of the Gaza Strip live.

I asked, "Can you indicate the rate among different sectors in children with mental disorders, such as children who are afraid of darkness or who have anxiety, severe mental disorder or have experienced violence?" Dr. Owaida responded,

> There are no accurate percentages, only professional impressions. Research after the last war showed that there was a relationship of psychological stress with the existing disorders. We found that at least 38% of the children in the Gaza Strip suffer from PTSD. There were also those with symptoms of PTSD. Every child in the Gaza Strip suffers from one or two symptoms of PTSD. The most common symptoms are excessive excitation or fear, nightmares, and night urination.

> As for other disorders, no less important and dangerous than what is mentioned, for example, excessive activity and excess

movement indicate development of traumatic disorders. The excess movement in the child may be part of the symptoms, and the negative adaptation in the child is the result of the symptoms of traumatic experience. There also are symptoms that may be hidden, and a parent may believe that his son suffers from a second problem, when in fact, the origin of the traumatic experiences is the same.

These strikes are difficult to deal with because the situation continues to be problematic, the anxiety continues. I'll give you a simple example, "just to hear the sound of airplanes." This immediately explores the latent symptoms and re-activates them when the child is frightened. It's natural to make the connection of planes with bombing, and with a new war beginning.

"Can you inform us about the current situation in Gaza and its impact on the children psychologically, especially the drones, the lack of electricity and the farmers and lack of healthy food, the increase in contaminated food, and the child beggars in the Gaza Strip?" He replied,

How could the war end if the Gaza Strip is still besieged by air, land, and sea? You are in prison. We are besieged, in prison and occupied, and the simplest types of freedoms have been confiscated. Until a person lives in dignity, we are still under pressure, which takes different forms.

There is no doubt for any Palestinian, even the child, that the Israeli occupation continues to practice the utmost torture against the Palestinian people through the impoverishment of the Palestinian people, and through lack of assistance obtaining important materials for industry and trade.

There is no job opportunity. The student cannot go out to get a scholarship, or even go to visit one of his relatives. I'm in a siege. The state of siege is another form of war practiced by the occupation but takes a psychological character.

Dr. Owaida suggested that part of the Israeli strategy was to make Palestinian people feel helpless, to defeat and control them more easily. This idea is rooted in the theory of learned helplessness, which was conceptualized and developed by American psychologist Martin Seligman.[175] He stated:

> I think that the occupation practices all kinds of experiences in Gaza, for example, when it destroys a person who is totally incapable of coping psychologically, that is what is meant by feeling helpless. Feeling helpless is psychological warfare, feeling that you have no value, you cannot be more than what the occupation wants you to be. This is a fundamental point of the psychological concept, called "Learned Helplessness," on how to create a helpless person.
>
> Look at the difficult social phenomena experienced by the Gaza Strip in cases of depression. Suicide cases. These suicides are a precedent for the Gaza Strip despite the different culture. All these factors are sought by the occupation and are a real result of the ongoing siege. Thus, the state of siege is another form of psychological pressure exerted on the Gaza Strip which generates a state of exhaustion on the psychological level.
>
> When you feel that there is no hope for you in the future, there is no hope for you to work after you finish university, there is no hope of living a normal life by associating with the woman you love, because you do not have all the ingredients, there is no house, there is no room, there is no hope, a person reaches the stage that it is better to die.
>
> Even the religious factor, which is supposed to be one of the most important factors of psychological rigidity, will be affected in one form or another. This explains the increase and frequency of suicide attempts, some of which were unfortunately successful.
>
> Therefore, this is an essential part of the goal of the occupation. The culture is affected by the environment you live in. If you

---

[175] Maier & Seligman, 1976.

measure the number of suicides five years or ten years ago and
now, you find a huge increase.

Hassan Zeyada is a mental health worker at the GCMHP and a
colleague of Dr. Owaida. He has seen and treated Palestinians suffering
from the psychological effects of Israeli occupation. He related to the
sense of impending doom that accompanied Israeli attacks on civilians
and social institutions:

> The Israeli military aggression in 2014 was a painful and scary
> experience for all Palestinians. What distinguished this Israeli
> military aggression was the people's insecurity and the awareness
> that every group of Palestinian society was targeted. That the
> people close to them or responsible for them may be targeted,
> created a state of concern for everyone.

> The Israeli aggression was greater than ever, targeting, shelling,
> and demolishing all components of society. They targeted all
> the factors of resilience or protection that the Palestinian human
> being had, seeking to destroy Palestinian ability to endure the
> strikes, and to crush any resilience in Palestinian society. They
> targeted schools and social institutions that provide humanitarian
> services, even mosques and the United Nations Relief and Works
> Agency (UNRWA) for the Palestinian people. They even targeted
> the Palestinian family, which is the most important source of
> support for the Palestinian. The result of this aggression was
> that 143 families lost an average of three members of the family.

As others have, Hassan emphasized the difference between earlier
Israeli aggressions and the 2014 attacks, and how the psychological effects
were serious and are probably long-term.

> This was different from the previous aggression. There was
> targeting within all areas of the Gaza Strip in full. No one was
> excluded, not the border areas, not the residential buildings,
> not the towers. This is a very important part. People left their

place of residence under threat and shelling and were unable to determine their destination because there was no safe place in the Gaza Strip during the aggression, which lasted 55 days.

All of this has created psychological effects that meant direct and long-term psychological problems, in multiple categories. In the course of the aggression most members of the Palestinian family suffered fear, anxiety, and sleep problems. Annoying dreams were present in the children; some had night urination, stuttering, increased movement and difficulty in attention and concentration. This was a primary complaint after the end of the Israeli aggression. We received some cases that were severely affected.

In adults there was a feeling of tension and anxiety which was reflected in their communication and the inability to withstand any frustrations. Some demonstrated verbal aggression, and some had severe physical complaints they were unable to bear; some had to use medicines as relief from this pain, to sleep during or after the aggression. Some got into the cycle of misusing medications to calm down tension, anxiety, and extreme fear that existed. This concerned people dear to the afflicted, for example, the mother or father had a concern for their children but were unable to secure a safe place or even protect them during the night. Even the decisions that were made in the family reflected the overall sense of doom that pervaded. If a bombing happened, let it happen to the entire family, they reasoned. Therefore, the entire family would sleep in the same place all together in case of a bombing, so that the family wouldn't be so sad if they lost one member. They would die all together. Because they could not imagine losing each other or feeling alone and sad.

I think the main part of these symptoms were post-traumatic stress disorder in adults and a high rate of depression in children. Symptoms in children included incontinence, urination at night, disorders in communication, and academic problems. Teachers complained of students' lack of attention. People agree now that there is a greater treatment effort needed to accomplish what was previously accomplished. What previously required half an hour or an hour now needs several hours because victims exhibit a problem in attention, which is the result of traumatic experiences during the aggression, bombing, and destruction. Some were directly exposed; some heard and saw things indirectly. Either way, we began to see this common characteristic in various groups in this community.

Long-Term Psychological Impacts

Limited research exists regarding the enduring psychological effects and mental well-being of individuals following traumatic events. For instance, a study in the Gaza Strip discovered that initially, 40% of children met criteria for probable Post-Traumatic Stress Disorder (PTSD), but this decreased to approximately 10% one year later, as peace processes commenced. While a child's initial exposure to war-related trauma may have been confined to a specific time and place, the aftermath of war introduces a range of ongoing stressors affecting both the child and their family. These secondary stressors include economic and social disruption, loss of loved ones, malnutrition, and illness. [176]

According to an article by Jon Shaw, a study conducted by Arpad Barath on children in Sarajevo in 1999 (four years after the war), found that most children continued to live in impoverished communities with compromised social infrastructure, leading to dangerous and unhealthy conditions such as overcrowding and unsafe playgrounds. Most of these children felt unsafe in their neighborhoods, faced challenges in school, and often fell ill. Nevertheless, many of these children displayed adaptive coping strategies in response to these stressors. [177]

Another study found that 43% of Lebanese children still exhibited post-traumatic stress symptoms a decade after experiencing war-related traumatic events. The biological impact of war-related traumas is closely tied to their severity, duration, and their effects on bodily integrity, the stress response system, and life-sustaining support systems. Research shows

---

[176] Thabet and Vostanis, 2000.

[177] Shaw, 2003.

that exposure to intense acute and chronic stress during developmental years can lead to enduring neurobiological effects, including increased risk of anxiety and mood disorders, problems with impulse control, compromised immune function, medical issues, structural changes in the central nervous system, and even premature death.[178]

Despite the compelling evidence linking exposure to war and violence with elevated stress levels and the development of PTSD symptoms, research has not adequately explored the effects of these experiences on the mental health of children in Middle Eastern countries, such as Iraq. The widespread exposure to potentially traumatic events in Iraq has inflicted long-lasting physical and psychological harm on both children and adults. According to the World Health Organization (WHO), over half a million children in Iraq may require clinical assistance, including psychotherapy. Furthermore, an estimated 10% of the approximately 5.7 million Iraqi children attending primary and secondary schools may urgently need psychotherapy due to their exposure to highly dangerous events with the potential to induce trauma.[179] The extensive effects of recurring trauma are distinct from those of a single traumatic incident. Palestinian children are continuously experiencing varied and repetitive trauma. How does this affect them?

Do such events inevitably lead to a deterioration in mental health, or can individuals develop resilience and coping mechanisms in response? Some suggest that, due to continual exposure to such events, children may develop a form of 'psychological immunization' that fosters resilience.[180] However, this viewpoint is not without its complexities and uncertainties.[181] Nevertheless, survivors of physical injuries in the Palestinian population, as I have personally witnessed in interviews, also strive to navigate the challenges of their mental well-being in various ways." Asmaa, for instance, gained confidence through talking. "Through talking, I had

---

[178] Freh, 2015.

[179] WHO, 2014.

[180] Okasha & Elkholy, 2012, p. 176.

[181] Freh, 2015.

the opportunity to release the feelings I have inside of me. I have no one but my kids and my husband, and God willing they stay well and around me." As we shall see in the following chapter, some of the victims like Asmaa explained how they have survived through a combination of their own resolve and will to live, as well as the support they were provided by refugee and assistance programs.

CHAPTER 5:

"I will continue to provide support to these families who have experienced a similar tragedy to mine"

How do the Palestinian people cope with life in a war zone? It is beyond the comprehension of people from safe, sovereign countries and cultures to understand what life has become for the survivors in Gaza. However, in the traumatic situation of the Gaza Strip, Palestinian children have demonstrated remarkable resilience by employing a spectrum of coping mechanisms to confront the profound trauma that engulfs their lives. These adaptive strategies serve as a testament to their unwavering determination to retain a semblance of control, hope, and psychological fortitude amid the adversities they face.[182] [183] Foremost among these coping strategies is the pursuit of social support, including the nurturing from family, the company of trusted friends, and the collective strength of their community. In a milieu marked by conflict and turmoil, these relationships become vital anchors.[184]

Simultaneously, many of these young people find solace and respite in creative outlets such as art, music, storytelling, and play, drawing sustenance from the wellspring of their cultural and religious identities. These artistic endeavors not only afford them an avenue for emotional expression but also provide therapeutic sanctuary.[185] Some children also have the privilege of accessing mental health care professionals through

[182] Bronfenbrenner, U. (2005)

[183] Khamis, V. (2011)

[184] Panter-Brick, C., et al. (2015)

[185] Thabet, A., et al. (2015)

local organizations and non-governmental entities. These dedicated practitioners employ a spectrum of mental health interventions tailored to the unique needs of the children, including community-based programs, trauma-focused therapies, and crucial support mechanisms for parents and caregivers.[186]

In Gaza, ways to persevere have evolved over time and after repeated incidents that bring death and destruction. Hassan Zeyada agrees with other survivors and mental health professionals that the political solution is the only way to truly improve mental health and all health:

> As a professional, I see that this reality is the outcome of political reality and without a political solution or political decisions to challenge and change this reality, a large group of people will suffer. As mental health workers we try to do our best to help people overcome this reality. I repeat, as professionals we do our best to help the victims of the Israeli violations and the ongoing aggression on the Gaza strip. We do not have any guarantee that Israeli occupation will never make another aggressive attack on the Gaza Strip and it might be more difficult the next time, and more catastrophic.

> We are talking about the victims or survivors of Israeli violations, so, we need as professionals in this area, to talk about the occupation and the aggressor, as well. It is good to care about the victims and to help them, but who can stop this aggression? As mental health workers we do our best to help people overcome the psychological and social consequences of this reality. But sometimes this effort is weak because of the repeated Israeli attacks. There is no guarantee that the occupation will not repeat these aggressions and violations and thus force the survivors and the victims of the Israeli attacks to return to mental health institutions for more treatment.

> We are talking about the aggressor, the occupation and its practices. Who will prevent the occupation from carrying

---

[186] Thabet A.A.M., et al. (2019)

out these practices again? Who will provide protection to the Palestinian society from these violations? We need a political dimension because this is the result of a political reality. We need to exert pressure as professional mental health workers. We cannot separate psychological health from respect for human rights and there are violations of human rights. Therefore, our efforts also stand in the direction that this political reality must be changed. The Israeli occupation must end so that people can live a life of stability, security, development, freedom of movement and respect for human rights.

The biggest violation of human rights is the Israeli occupation, and therefore I believe that there is a direct relationship between this reality and the improvement of mental health. We are doing our best, but this repeated demolition of Palestinian people and communities by the Israeli attacks must be stopped, regardless of method. Because you cannot build up and at the same time destroy someone. But this aggression won't end, and each new aggression becomes much stronger and more violent. Therefore, the homes demolished, the people wounded and martyred, all this cannot continue. We need to put an end to the Israeli occupation. Then we can talk about a real and continuous improvement in the level of mental health of the people in the Gaza Strip and the occupied territories.

Coping Style

Wahdan discussed with me how survivors were told of their relatives' deaths. I asked, "How did your children react to the loss of their mother, the loss of your legs, and their own injuries?"

As for these kids," Wahdan said, "they didn't find anyone to support them, meaning their aunt was injured, the aunts-in-law were injured as well. People who are not related to us were the ones who stood with them. They (Musab, Omar, and Mohammed) had two other aunts who lived in Khan Yunis.

One of their aunts went with them to Turkey. They did not know anyone. All their family members were either killed or injured. Their aunts-in-law, their aunt, their uncles, cousins who were with us in Beit Hanoun, all were injured in the same house we were in.

"How did the children accept the loss of their mother?"

Slowly, slowly. Musab was the oldest of them and he was four and a half years old. He was asking about his father—they told him that the Israelis imprisoned him. His aunt-in-law would close the door of the house on him so he would not run away. Then slowly, slowly they told him 'Your mother was killed'. Afterward, they told him 'Your father is okay now and he would like to speak to you. He is in Egypt'. And he started to call me on the phone. But these children were a year and a half old and three years old, they did not know who their father and mother were.

This one stayed with his uncle and his uncle's wife. She became like a mother figure for him. But Musab is the one who had it hard, he was missing his mother and father. I stayed for almost four months in Egypt for treatment; it was so difficult for him.

Wa'd found that drawing was her only escape from the gloom:

We fled the area hoping that we are going to a safe place, my grandfather's house, but the bombing was everywhere and in the entire area. So, afterward, we went to the school. They told us we would be safe there at the school. The situation in the schools was very bad, diseases were spread, and crowded. People were on top of each other, the room has more than fifty people, mixed boys, girls, and families. The place itself was not comfortable. I had to wear my headscarf and my full garment for 24 hours.

At the schools, I used to feel lonely, I did not feel psychologically comfortable. Unfortunately, we had to live that gloomy reality. For me, I like drawing, it was the only way! I draw and I unload what I feel through drawing. This was the only thing that helped me during the war.

Dr. Kamal Qadih knows that youth need some respite, some place to think:

> In addition to the populated areas in Khuza'a, there are agricultural areas. These agricultural areas are considered a breathing space for children, where they can go for fresh air, play and vent their hearts to rid them of the economic, security and social problems.

Um Hani shared her sadness in therapy sessions. I asked her, "Do you have a close friend who you can talk to? Has any one of the psychological health workers ever come to talk to you?" She answered:

> Sadness is a natural feeling in such a situation. Sadness over the martyrdom of my son and the destruction. And the sorrow of those around me and what they suffered. Where on the same day my son was martyred, his close friend from our neighbor was killed and buried next to him.

Um Hani lost everything and still awaits any compensation. "You lost a child, money, a living, and a home," I observed to begin our conversation. "The Israelis destroyed your life in all aspects."

"That's exactly what happened to me. I am the most damaged person in this area. It is possible that the loss of homes and livelihoods will be compensated, but my son is gone."

"You were destroyed socially, health-wise and economically," I acknowledged. "When you left the hospital and after your son was killed, may he rest in peace, did you come back to your home in the truce?" Um Hani answered:

> I could not return here at the same time because I could not bear to see where my son was martyred and see his blood in the place of destruction. When I returned, I went to live with my relative in a school accommodation center for 15 days. I never

went to see my house. I told my son that I cannot bear to see the place where his brother died or the extent of the destruction.

But after a while, I decided to go to see what happened. I actually went to sit on the ruins of the destroyed house and cry. This was his jalabaya (garment) and these are his pants and this was his bed. Honestly, it was a real disaster.

"During the war, did you ever feel afraid of death?" I asked. "A feeling that you might lose your family?"

"My son called me from Libya to find out what happened to us. I told him you should be prepared at any moment to hear the news of the martyrdom of any of us, whether me or his father or his brother. Because it was a crazy war."

"When you returned to the area did you feel nervous?"

It was not just nerves or shock but a complete nervous breakdown. People around me were talking to me and I was completely astray. Until this moment, my mind has been displaced and I keep retrieving the memories. My son's memories when he was among us. Sometimes when I sit alone, I remember what happened and I weep hard.

"On the psychological level, in your daily actions, do you feel nervous?"

No. But I became closer with family members and spread love and sympathy between us. So much so that, one of my sons wanted to separate from us and rent a house to live in but I refused and asked him to stay by my side because I cannot live with a sense of longing for him.

Wael realized life would not be easy for his disabled son. "How do you deal with your new situation with your amputated legs?" I asked him. Wael replied:

It is true that my life is different, but I adapted to it. My legs were amputated but I walk and move. The problem is with this little child whose leg has been amputated and also his eye is gone. Thinking about his future and how he grows up, and how he is among the other children, how do they go to school and kindergarten? If someone pushed him strongly in school it might be the end of school for him. It will become a psychological problem growing up, and his eye will remain gone.

Hassan Zeyada, a mental health worker at the GCMHP, sees more acceptance of mental health treatment than in the past, noting that the stigma attached to it has largely been shed, due to families no longer losing their reputation over having a member in treatment:

I think there is acceptance of mental health services and psychological treatment. This is what I noted through the changes that have taken place in the Palestinian society in the Gaza Strip. I have been working in the field since 1991. In general, there is an improvement in the trend of community members receiving mental health services. Stigma was most severe among various groups in Palestinian society in the early 1990s at the beginning of the first Intifada. But nowadays we can say there is an improvement.

Receiving services is more relatable to people if the suffering and repercussions of the psychological situation result from violence related to the occupation. Therefore, people have the ability to express the repercussions of this experience, as long as it's a result of the practices of the Israeli occupation attacks, incursions and violations. But there is an improvement. If we review GCMHP records about the sources of transformation, we see that the family became part of the conversion by making their own decision. Records reveal that Palestinian families decided that receiving mental health services was a positive, life affirming choice.

There is still some stigma associated with mental health services and its workers, and people prefer not to work in this field. Sensitivity to stigma is still linked to mental health issues that affect the reputation of the family or individuals in society. It is less present. But we still need to increase awareness and knowledge and reduce sensitivity during the receipt of these services because many hesitate to make the decision, and delaying the decision to take the appropriate services in a timely manner leads to more complex problems, which makes it even more difficult to deal with.

I think there is a change. Today we can see categories that receive our services. We have educated university students, workers, and housewives. Large groups of Palestinian society receive these services including university students, people with education and positions in the community, housewives, children and grade-school students. Therefore, this is a change to the direction of mental health services in general. Some are preparing to consult through the GCMHP helpline. This addresses the stigma and sensitivity that exists in the culture, and in facing psychological problems, and this helps to educate people and give accurate and correct information on mental health. It is also possible that the first step is that people decide to receive services in our specialized centers in the Gaza Strip.

During our conversation, I asked Hassan to tell me about his personal experiences during the 2014 war and how his job played a role in helping people. He replied:

The recent Israeli military aggression on Gaza was a painful experience. During this aggression I lost six members of the family, my mother and three of my brothers, and I lost my nephew and my brother's wife. During this aggression the family house was a four-story building completely bombed without prior warning. Personally, as a human being and as a professional in this field, my reaction was a normal reaction, a sense of shock.

At first, I was unable to recognize and accept this experience. I could not contain my feelings of sadness and pain at the loss of these people who are dearly, distinctly personal to me. My pain and sadness extended to the remaining families of my brothers, and to my wife and children. But this sadness we were dealing with is human feeling, and this was my reaction towards those who belong to me, a natural reaction to grieve, cry and remember. I had problems adapting because of the loss, and as a result of the imbalance which happened to the whole family.

But there was also support that existed clearly within the family. Everyone who has a social relationship with us as a family was a source of support. The most important support I received was from my wife. She is also primarily a psychologist working in the same field. I also received support by supervision from the staff of the Gaza Community Mental Health Program.

Hassan represents a new normal in Palestine that attempts to accept what has happened to him, and to others, as events that are prone to happen due to the current hostile circumstances. This sad truth is courageously adopted as another survival technique. He told me:

I also tried to accept this reality, and to take responsibility for what resulted from the loss inside my family. I have contributed by offering help for family members to feel and deal with this loss and their existing reactions as normal. There was a common decision among all members of the family, including me, that this is normal, and it won't stop us from continuing the track that was planned, whether as students of schools or universities, or on the level of social responsibility. This decision that I took to take responsibility for follow-up care and secure all the requirements of the family within the support of the whole family gave me satisfaction. Despite all the feelings of grief and loss that existed, we tried to continue along naturally and to share these normal and acceptable feelings and sensibilities.

We can still continue to maintain all these paths and visions of the future life which was planned by our family, which was a part of our dreams. The first step was to secure the basic needs of family members. Four of our families became homeless. One brother, his wife and son, left four daughters and a child. The second brother left three children, a daughter and his wife. The third brother left two children and his wife. There was a basic duty to support the extended family by securing basic needs and by being a source of support in all matters.

Hassan's own personal tragedy led him to recognize his ability to help others and guide them through their personal catastrophes. He recalls what he deems natural responses, and how they helped him, and how he used them to help others:

The second thing I discovered is that my practical and previous knowledge contributed to understanding these reactions on the personal level, and at the level of my children, and at the level of the sisters and brothers who remained from the family, and their children. This helped me to offer support as a father and as a brother to the family members, and not as a professional. But this experience has helped me to increase my understanding, knowledge and awareness of the psychological suffering that many families face. Therefore, my knowledge helped sharpen my ability to communicate with understanding and genuine empathy with families who lost family members.

This makes me more professional and closer to these families in helping them overcome the repercussions of their losses. I think it helped me to overcome this issue. I also kept on doing my role and work. I continued to make my fieldwork follow-up visits and psychological interventions after the end of the war. This gave me energy, satisfaction, and a feeling that I could live on and grow despite my suffering, even as I continue to get older and still miss my family and feel sad.

I saw them in my dreams and I remember them every day and this is a human feeling and I will not deny these human feelings. I hope that my experience will help me more and I will continue to provide support to these families who have experienced a similar tragedy as mine. In this difficult and painful reality in the Gaza Strip, with the siege and Israeli violations and repeated aggression, and all the repercussions of this—unemployment, inability to travel, all the problems of daily life, of power and water cuts, even with all these things, we try to contribute to further enhance this ability of people to agree with this reality.

Enas is a psychologist at the GCMHP and a colleague of Hassan and Dr. Owaida. I asked her, "Through your experience after 2014, and working with children in particular, what are the changes you noticed as a psychologist for Palestinian children in the Gaza Strip? What is different psychologically when comparing the 2014 war to previous factors and aggression such as 2008 and 2012?" Enas responded:

The children were affected because they were the main victims in every war, the most vulnerable group in the society, so they suffered and still suffer from the effects of war. Each war has its own specificity and differences, but the last war of 2014 was more violent because it invaded the entire Gaza Strip. All places for people in general were unsafe. Those who had previous experience in the wars of 2012 and 2008 and were directly attacked or left their homes had alternative plans. But by 2014 all plans changed because even the safest places, for example, the towers, were attacked directly. Therefore, the first thing that happened to children was that safety became real only in their imagination. Trust is not there anymore. We could be victims at any time, with no protection.

Therefore, their loss of safety has led them to be vulnerable to most psychological symptoms. They are different and variable, and even using the diagnostic medicine book we have no clear method to diagnose the total number and types of symptoms in Gaza. It means that we suffer from continuous shocks and need more explanation and study.

For example, in the Second Intifada we saw children display a "rush" (meaning the opposite of avoidance, which we consider to be a symptom of psychological trauma). They used to throw stones directly at the enemy. This became more difficult to watch in the Second Intifada because the children faced the military hardware, but without fear. Despite the fact that the children had no fear, in psychology their confrontational behavior is called a "rush" of fear. The subject becomes more ambiguous to the children. The war is not present and the enemy is not clear, but they will attack by hidden means, so the children have more fear, more anticipation, and more pain.

The persistent exposure to violence experienced by Palestinians leads to complex methods of coping. Their unique circumstances, marked by ongoing violence, forced displacement, and profound loss, have compelled them to develop adaptive coping mechanisms and strategies for mental survival. As suggested by Fathi et al., the constant threat of violence forces individuals to adapt by developing strategies to maintain psychological and physiological balance.[187] As suggested by Yablon (2001), the thrill experienced during violent incidents can help victims maintain psychological and physiological equilibrium, providing a sense of control amidst chaos.[188] Among these, children in particular may develop a desensitization to violence and form unusual attachments to it. This can be explained by the fact that the sensation of excitement derived from these experiences can serve as a means for victims to maintain their psychological and physiological equilibrium. However, over time, they may become excessively comfortable in highly stimulating and perilous environments.[189]

---

[187] Fathi, Bakr, & Gharaibeh, 2013.

[188] Yablon, 2001.

[189] Yablon, 2001.

Moreover, constant exposure to violence during childhood can lead to neurophysiological alterations with far-reaching consequences. Research by Qouta et al., suggests that early and severe exposure to violence can profoundly affect children's neurological development, potentially altering their threshold for aggression and impacting their ability to empathize with others. This can create a cycle of violence, as children raised in such environments may be more prone to perpetuate it in the future.[190] The constant exposure to violence that Palestinians, especially children, endure has given rise to complicated coping mechanisms and neurophysiological changes. While these coping mechanisms may initially serve as a means of survival, they can have long-term detrimental effects on individuals and society. Consequently, immediate intervention and support are crucial to break the cycle of violence, enabling Palestinian children to develop healthier coping strategies and fostering empathy and resilience for a better future.

Enas has focused on family bonds and on restoring family relationships to aid children in recovering from severe shocks they have experienced in the bombing and killing. He has learned to recognize children's symptoms as reactions to the unresolved shock and maintains hope that—even as normalcy is denied by lack of future opportunities—a child's soul still infuses his life.

Most of the parents said that their children's academic achievement was much better in the past. People thought they forgot about the war of 2014, and after a year or two they forgot about the effects of war, but the symptoms are present in children. Withdrawn socially, or violent with the other children. We must keep in mind that they are just children shocked by the war, and therefore still suffering because of the integration of the problem of war and fear, which becomes a personality, no matter what way the child expresses his pain. It is difficult to change the reality; however, all the children are not psychotic because the child still fights and lives his life. He goes to school

---

[190] Qouta, Punamäki, & El Sarraj, 2008.

and does his homework, and he loves playing with his friends. The soul of life is still there.

However, life is suffering if we want to talk about post-traumatic stress disorder. It means that there is a defect in the normal functioning of the child, but the imbalance means what happened to the children is a complete defect. Many cases differ from others but are all affected by the surrounding situation, the symptoms of disability and fear of losing hope. In the Palestinian children these things have become part of the personality. As a child they say: "What is the future?" I do not know. "Why do I have to work while the graduate has no work?" I hear people's daily complaints about life's daily pressure and the children. "What's the goal of education? My brother who's educated and unemployed?"

Meanwhile, after the last war, children or parents do not notice symptoms of trauma or war symptoms directly. It comes indirectly, by complaining. Problems in the clinic are unintentional urination or sleep problems in children, nightmares, uncontrolled moving or having epilepsy, academic problems, and violence. This child is not the child of the past. The system data clearly states that this child is full of symptoms, post-traumatic stress disorder.

There are different symptoms, and the history of the problem's origin becomes the history of this child, how the pregnancy progressed, how his natural growth compared to his normal sister's, how main events of his life passed and if this child was exposed to anything dangerous. But if there is a particular event in his house with his family, with a different child, this child will be affected and we will look step by step, because we know that has much impact on him. As a specialist with children who have experienced repeated trauma, I face a great challenge in this treatment when the symptoms are not complete or clear for the child who has experienced shock, so we take the whole family history.

The observations gathered from the Rought-Brooks study underscore a profound reality. While assessing the psychological support afforded to their children, interviewees articulated poignant narratives. One mother talked about faith. "The children stopped having faith in us as parents," she said. "My children can see that their mother can't protect them. We were wondering when we would die. The children are now getting better."[191] Another interviewee affirmed, "The provision of psychological support is instrumental in fostering the recovery of our children." [192] However, even within the trajectory of recuperation, these children confront an exorbitant burden, grappling not only with their own traumatic experiences but also shouldering the weight of their parents' unresolved trauma. A mother from Rafah articulated her ongoing psychological struggles showing how her unresolved distress manifested in the form of vented frustration upon her children: "As an adult, I find myself in dire need of psychological assistance. Each passing day, I deal with the realization that my ability to manage anger diminishes, and my emotions are unintentionally transferred onto my children." [193] This example, among many, show that the enduring impact of traumatic experiences, especially within familial dynamics, necessitates an empathetic and comprehensive approach to psychological healing and recovery.

Enas acknowledges the losses in the children's lives, as well as her own. Social norms and traditions have been destroyed and social groups and meetings have disappeared, making it even harder to establish support for mental health treatment. He said:

> We observe the extent of the suffering of the child and the extent of the direct trauma of the war and try to connect them. If we pay attention to the child and work through education, with parents, and follow the school in trying to alleviate the symptoms in children, we can handle the changing situation as a psychological treatment. But we will highlight that this

---

[191] Rought-Brooks, 2015, p. 44

[192] Rought-Brooks, 2015, p. 44

[193] Rought-Brooks, 2015, p. 45

child is suffering from a growing void. We are adults and our suffering, also from a growing void, is reflected. So, we try to return to the routine at the beginning of the family, we return to relationships. For example, if the child suffers from problems from the absence of the father at home, and the lack of interest in his relationship with his children, and there is no dialogue, and the mother is irritable, and there are many burdens in her life so there is no dialogue with the child, we start there.

When we were able to get the parents' attention back on the child, and as we worked to highlight the child, the symptoms started to get worse because when he was ready, he lived, but the hardest of the family did not give him attention, so the shock was harder. The idea in Gaza is that, we are more capable of getting rid of or minimizing the symptoms of the ongoing trauma if we return to the Palestinian family system, which was the goal. We are shocked, for example, that the neighbor isn't seeing his neighbor anymore. Now, the social communication we had in our old time and gave us a boost no longer occurs because the people are not in their old groups to share their experiences and relieve themselves. This is a chance to alleviate the symptoms of trauma by trying to help them in the clinic to take greater care of the child.

I agreed and prompted, "In the previous wars we had family reunification and social solidarity, but in 2014 that was targeted." Enas replied:

Being together has been targeted by the Intifada. The violence has become more and more intolerable, combined with pressure through wars and siege and high unemployment. Palestinian families average five children, or seven in Shuja'iyya. They are aware of the high unemployment rate and it creates pressure in the family itself. There is no tolerance left in the family. Pressure from all sides is no longer bearable. For example, before the 2009 war there were invasions in Beit Hanoun in 2006. In Beit Hanoun there were invasions and people dying, but in Gaza

City we had no idea about what was happening, we had our own pressures.

For example, there was an invasion in the Zeitoun neighborhood in the border areas but, as to the feelings of the people of Gaza, it barely existed. They are numb. Feelings exist but it's difficult for a man to bear a long-lived idleness. Violence had completely overtaken all of us in 2014. There are no longer psychological defenses estimated to protect us, but one can protect his soul and be in an appropriate place and have safety.

If you ask anyone in the street, where will you flee in the next war? He is going to tell you that he will stay where he is because nowhere is safe. There is a burning pressure. The Israeli enemy is already running the game because they can press and control and impose the closure of Gaza. They exert pressure on us from all directions. People are affected by the violence and anger from all directions and react naturally to the situation.

In a comprehensive investigation undertaken by esteemed scholars of psychological health at Gaza Islamic University entitled *Psychological Indicators of Drawings by Palestinian Children After the Gaza War*, an examination of Palestinian children's drawings in the aftermath of the Gaza War was conducted. The study unveiled a distressing reality, with a staggering 82.3% of the surveyed children crafting illustrations entwined with conflict. Fighter planes against a backdrop of crumbling homes and mosques, depictions of rockets and Israeli missiles, lifeless Palestinian figures, military apparata, and armed militants were all present in their work.[194] In one example, Malak Abu Jamous, who witnessed the tragic loss of her beloved grandfather, drew "a variety of things in the past: a plane bombing, a child dying, a demolished house."[195] In a heartrending interview with Al Jazeera, Malak unveiled her latest creation—a modest dwelling with an elderly gentleman standing beside it. "This is my grandfather,

---

[194] Abou-Dagga, 2013.

[195] Al-Haddad, 2017, "Malak Abu Jamous," para. 1.

Salman, and this is me," she said.[196] The child's artwork became a conduit for her emotions and evidence of the effects of the conflict on her psyche. This study further explained the participants' experiences of emotional and psychological vulnerability during the Israeli offensive of 2014. The testimonials woven into their artwork and discussions, provided a window into the scars borne by the children in the aftermath of conflict.

The American Heritage Dictionary defines emotion as "a psychological state that arises spontaneously rather than through conscious effort and is sometimes accompanied by physiological changes; a feeling."[197] Emotions are complex and multifaceted psychological experiences that play a crucial role in human life. They encompass a wide range of feelings, including joy, sadness, anger, fear, and love, among others. Emotions are integral to how humans perceive and respond to the world around them, influencing their thoughts, behaviors, and interactions with others. The spontaneous nature of emotions implies that they often occur without conscious effort or control. For instance, one may feel a surge of happiness upon receiving good news or experience fear when confronted with a threatening situation. These emotional responses arise automatically, reflecting the brain's intricate processes in assessing and reacting to various stimuli. Moreover, emotions are closely linked to physiological changes in the body. When an individual experiences intense emotion, such as fear or anger, the body can respond with increased heart rate, heightened alertness, and changes in hormone levels. This physiological component of emotion underscores the interconnectedness of mind and body in emotional experiences.

Researchers from various fields, including psychology, neuroscience, and philosophy, have explored the nature of emotions extensively. The study of emotions has led to various theories and models that seek to explain their origins, functions, and effects on human behavior. Prominent theories, such as the James-Lange theory, Cannon-Bard theory, and Schachter-Singer theory, offer different perspectives on how emotions

---

[196] Al-Haddad, 2017, "Malak Abu Jamous," para. 1.

[197] American Heritage Dictionary, 2021.

arise and their relationship with physiological responses.[198] [199] [200] Emotions are integral to human experience and have a profound impact on how individuals perceive and navigate the world. Therefore, understanding participants' emotions that accrued during the war contributes to our understanding of their behavior, cognition, and well-being.

The study cited above, *Psychological Indicators of Drawings by Palestinian Children After the Gaza War,* presented findings from the participants' verbatim narratives of their lived experiences of war trauma, which included emotional responses to witnessing war. Participants' exposure to war most often manifested in fear, terror, confusion, trauma, helplessness, and powerlessness. Participants had experienced a wide and extreme range of war events during the Israeli war on Gaza in 2014, which they described as "narrowly escaping death," "thinking that they would be killed," and "barely ran for their life," among others. Others talked about witnessing "parents being killed," "siblings being killed," "neighbors being killed," "homes being bombed," "seeing the bodies or parts of the bodies of the persons who had been killed," "witnessing their village or refugee camp being raided by the Israeli army and beating or killing of Palestinians," "suffering from hunger," "lack of clean water," "no power," "nowhere to escape," "death everywhere," "no place is safe," and so on. One participant talked about his experience being directly bombed: "We came back and the Israelis shelled the house ... they bombed the house while we were still inside it, my head was injured and open." His father described his son's experience:

> When they bombed the house, a rocket struck his head and opened from here, and his skull was broken, and his scalp got torn. This caused him huge psychological scars ... now he is receiving psychological therapy, but his condition is getting worse every day. These are the effects of the war.

---

[198] LeDoux, 1996.

[199] Cannon, 1927.

[200] Schachter, & Singer, 1962.

Another child described a similar experience: "The drones and the Israelis started shelling us and I was injured in my stomach." Another girl described her experience of her family being hit by a missile: "Suddenly a rocket came towards me, the missile came and suffocated us all with gas. We could not escape...Then a missile hit my brother and he died. Splinters of the missile hit my hand."

These children's accounts of their traumatic experiences underscore the severe psychological and emotional toll that Palestinian children endure, where they are exposed to violence, injury, and the loss of loved ones. Such traumatic events can have profound and lasting effects on their mental well-being, leading to psychological challenges, including post-traumatic stress disorder (PTSD), anxiety, and depression. These narratives highlight the urgent need for interventions to end this conflict, provide peace and safety to Palestinian children, provide support systems to address the psychological distress experienced by them and cope with their traumatic experiences, and work towards healing and recovery.

Family dynamics

The role of a close-knit family unit is a paramount safeguard for the psychological well-being of children.[201] Within war environments, children are forced to relinquish their innocence.[202] Confronting the horrors of war unavoidably inflicts psychological repercussions.[203] In the face of life-threatening situations, children often manifest their distress through anxiety, somatic complaints, and withdrawal. Particularly among the very young, a tendency to revert to earlier stages of development is observed, including gravitating towards their parents as a source of solace and security.

The Palestinian family structure has long occupied a pivotal and cherished position within the cultural fabric of Gaza. It has served as emotional sustenance, social cohesion, and economic resilience when

---

[201] Qouta & El Sarraj, 2002.

[202] El-Sarraj & Qouta, 2005, p. 233.

[203] Garbarino, Kostelny, & Dubrow, 1991b.

faced with adversity. However, the unrelenting barrage of Israeli conflicts has left an indelible mark on the familial bonds.

The Israeli-Palestinian conflict has subjected Gazan families to an incessant array of stressors, including forced displacement, economic hardship, the heartrending loss of loved ones, and constant insecurity. These hardships have challenged the traditional roles and functions of Palestinian families. In addition, the Israeli wars have had a toll on educational aspirations, stifled economic opportunities, and destroyed daily life. [204]

Operations Cast Lead in 2008-2009 and Protective Edge in 2014, characterized by widespread devastation and loss of life, have left a trail of traumatized families. These conflicts have severely disrupted the rhythm of everyday family life, through constant conflict, violence, and displacement, which has particularly scarred the children of Gaza. Many Palestinian children now bear the heavy burden of trauma and stress-related disorders, placing considerable strain on familial bonds. In their quest to provide emotional solace and a semblance of normalcy, parents find themselves in an ever-tightening web of familial instability.[205] [206]

The constant conflict, with its air raids, bombings, and the loss of loved ones, has given rise to a pandemic of psychological repercussions within Palestinian families. The unceasing violence and the erosion of safety have created pervasive psychological distress, disproportionately impacting the most vulnerable—children. This sustained trauma stifles healthy development. [207] Moreover, the loss of family members, whether due to casualties or imprisonment, has left a profound sense emptiness within Palestinian households. This emotional trauma acts as a corrosive force, undermining the bonds that traditionally hold families together, rendering family dynamics more fragile. The ceaseless threat of violence

[204] Abu Tawahina, 2018.

[205] Human Rights Watch, 2009.

[206] OCHA, 2021.

[207] Palestinian Center for Human Rights, 2020.

and the absence of a secure haven have cultivated an atmosphere of dread and anxiety within the family unit, further straining its resilience.

Moreover, the economic blockade imposed on Gaza has given rise to soaring levels of unemployment and poverty. These economic tribulations impose an immense burden on families, straining parents' ability to provide. In some cases, economic hardship compels family members to seek opportunities beyond Gaza, leading to physical separation which further exacerbates familial tensions. The ongoing Israeli blockade and military interventions have wreaked havoc on the Gazan economy, resulting in staggering unemployment rates, making necessities such as clean water, healthcare, and education rare luxuries.[208] Consequently, numerous Palestinian families in Gaza grapple with securing their basic needs, while dealing with intensifying financial stress and tension within the family. Economic destitution, stemming from Israeli trade restrictions and restricted mobility, has pushed many Palestinian families into poverty. Women in particular are compelled to assume more prominent roles in the workforce and as heads of households, effectively challenging societal norms.

The Israeli aggression in Gaza has undeniably taken a toll on every facet of Palestinian family life. It has thrown traditional familial dynamics into disarray, precipitated economic hardships, stretched relationships to their limits, and left a lasting psychological imprint on family members. Despite these tribulations, it is crucial to recognize the remarkable resilience of the Palestinian family in Gaza. Families persist in their duty to provide emotional support, care for one another, and preserve their cultural and social ties to the best of their abilities. In response to the psychological and economic challenges brought about by Israeli aggression, a burgeoning network of community support has emerged, providing families with a lifeline they sorely need.[209]

The Palestinian family, firmly established as a vital institution in Gaza, continues to stand as a cornerstone of stability and security for its members.

---

[208] UNRWA, 2021.

[209] UNRWA, 2021.

Nonetheless, the ceaseless Israeli aggression has forced the Palestinian family to adapt to the realities of life under occupation and conflict. The displacement of families, loss of homes, loss of family members, and the impact of conflict have created a complex backdrop for the people of Gaza. The families of Gaza epitomize extraordinary resilience in the face of relentless adversity. Families in Gaza draw strength from their deep-rooted cultural and familial ties. The extended family structure prevalent in the region provides a crucial support system. These families come together to share resources, emotional support, and solidarity amid the challenges. Community support networks, traditional coping mechanisms, and grassroots mental health initiatives are crucial components of their resistance against the psychological impact of adversity. Another aspect of their resilience is their ability to adapt to challenging circumstances. The prolonged conflict has forced families to develop innovative survival strategies, such as creating makeshift homes, utilizing alternative energy sources, and finding new ways to sustain their livelihoods. These adaptations showcase the families' determination to maintain a semblance of normalcy despite the harsh conditions. Despite facing significant challenges in accessing education, Gaza's families prioritize the learning and development of their children. Educational institutions become spaces of hope, where the resilience of families is reflected in their commitment to providing a better future for their children. Families invest in the education of their youth, fostering a sense of resilience that transcends generations. During my interview with Palestinian mothers, many spoke about the educational support they provide to their children after school due to their concerns over their children's ability to learn at school.

In contexts characterized by life-threatening circumstances, traumatic experiences, and war, the parental role of safeguarding children and fostering the development of their moral virtues is often impeded. This interference may precipitate a deterioration in familial relationships and potentially serve as a precursor to the emergence of aggressive and antisocial behaviors among the affected children.[210]

---

[210] Punamäki, 2009.

The family unit, even in the presence of conflict, assumes a vital role in giving children a sense of protection, solace, and inner resilience necessary to endure the perils and violence that surround them. Studies conducted with Palestinian families facing loss, injuries, and death, have underscored the significance of supportive and non-punitive parenting practices. These practices have proven instrumental in shielding children from the influence of aggressiveness.[211]

Palestinian mother Asmaa has tried healing and therapeutic programs, but her psychological and emotional wounds are too deep. She told me:

> It's impossible to come back to the life I led before. They took me to the women's affairs center. They told me to come and they would help me to set up a small pastries project to help support my family. I kept going for a while but I didn't get it. My sisters-in-law got it. I was hoping that (by) opening a little business I can help myself and my kids but I was out of luck. I stayed home disappointed because I was hoping that this project can support me and the children.

Even with this pain, Asmaa is a protector for her family. She must shield her daughter from hurtful teasing from other kids:

> My little child comes to me and starts crying, she tells me the kids said so and so: your breast has no nipple, when you get married, we need to get you a balloon or something. This is what the kids on the street say to her and she comes to me and starts crying. I get very saddened by this and by my child's situation.

War and trauma impose unique and arduous demands on family relationships and parental responsibilities. A study by Qouta et al. reveals a notable shift in the dynamics between parents and children within families scarred by violent trauma. This shift is accompanied by a gendered

---

[211] Qouta, Punamäki, Miller, and El Sarraj, 2008.

dimension in the parenting dynamics. Parents, in general, tend to adopt a stance of stern discipline, rejection, and at times, hostility, with mothers being more inclined towards highly punitive rearing practices. Importantly, this does not eclipse the underlying support and affection that children continue to experience from their parents.[212]

Gender emerges as a factor in this context, with the study revealing nuanced associations. Among boys, political engagement is correlated with supportive and affectionate fathering, whereas among girls, political involvement is linked to more punitive and restrictive maternal and paternal parenting styles. This underscores a universal tendency among parents to protect and restrict their daughters, while encouraging their sons to actively participate.[213]

Nevertheless, it remains indisputable that the family serves as a support in the lives of these children. The family symbolizes sanctuary, a source of comfort, and a haven of belonging: "Palestinian families in the Gaza Strip are large, 5-13 children on average, and people show strong affiliation to the family. *El Hamula* (the extended family) plays an important role both in protecting and obliging its members."[214]

Within Arab tradition, there is profound respect for the authority of parents, and the senior-most members of the family are held in the highest regard. However, military conflict and the trauma of displacement have, at times, strained the fabric of Palestinian society. During the first intifada, traditional family relationships and hierarchies were challenged due to the increasing influence of political parties, which diminished the social role of the extended family.

Furthermore, young people and children have assumed significant roles in the national struggle, often exceeding their parents' involvement. This has occasionally placed them in opposition to the wishes of their elders. The relentless cycle of violence and warfare has left parents feeling powerless in their attempts to shield their children from the ceaseless

---

[212] Qouta et al., 1995b (p. 317).

[213] Qouta et al., 1995b (p. 317).

[214] Qouta, Punamäki, & El Sarraj, 2008.

brutality, danger, and moral erosion of conflict. Conversely, children have witnessed the humiliation, vulnerability, suffering, and loss experienced by their parents. [215]

Resilience

Extensive evidence illustrates the profound impact of war on the physical and psychological well-being of children and adolescents, along with the substantial developmental challenges it imposes. Remarkably, amidst these harsh circumstances, children exposed to the ravages of conflict often exhibit resilience, enabling them to not only endure but even flourish in their developmental journey. The way violence shapes children's experiences is intrinsically tied to their interpretation and psychological processing of these experiences, as well as the various psychological and social factors accompanying them. [216]

Amid life-threatening situations, children may display tendencies toward aggression, driven by their diminished capacity to discern safer, neutral, and peaceful messages due to the prominence of war-related cognitive processing. Furthermore, the relationships between parents and children can be severely strained and imperiled by the pervasive violence of armed conflict. In such conditions, children are constantly exposed to external threats, which challenges parents to ensure their safety and security. In the absence of a secure environment, children may be inclined towards the development of aggressive behavior.

Increased exposure to war and military violence raises the risk of children manifesting aggressive tendencies, particularly when they perceive their parents as lacking affection or support, when parent-child interactions become marked by insecurity and fear, or when parents are no longer present. The likelihood of aggression rises when fundamental developmental milestones, such as the establishment of trust, emotional

---

[215] Qouta et al., 1995b.

[216] Barber, 2013; Boyden, 2003; Punamäki, 2009; Punamäki et al., 2001; Straker, 1992; Wessells, 1998.

regulation, and the formation of complex cognitive and moral judgments, are compromised. Additionally, a predisposition to aggressive behavior may emerge because of biased, inconsistent, and constrained emotional processing of distressing experiences.[217]

Nevertheless, human beings are characterized by their tenacity and resilience in the face of adversity. They demonstrate the capacity to adapt successfully, attain developmental competencies, overcome tribulations and trauma, construct meaningful life narratives through dynamic developmental processes, and ultimately thrive. Children subjected to war often exhibit remarkable endurance and resilience, evading any discernible signs of significant social or psychological impairment.[218]

It is essential, however, to recognize that while they may seem resilient, war-affected children are perpetually negotiating the delicate balance between resilience and vulnerability, courage and fear. This study provides insight into the transformative power of psychosocial support within Palestinian society, illustrating how strong family bonds can amplify resilience among participants. When individuals such as Musab, Omar, and Mohammed lost family members or endured injuries during the Israeli-Gaza conflict of 2014, the broader Palestinian community, often unrelated by blood, stepped forward to provide crucial support. Even when these individuals needed to seek medical treatment in Turkey for their war-related injuries, distant aunts residing in another town stood by their side. Astonishingly, despite the profound trauma they endured during the war, the participants' creativity and self-esteem remained unscathed.[219]

Early research posited the notion of "antifragility," suggesting that individuals, when confronted with stressors, exhibit an innate ability to maintain psychological equilibrium and emotional well-being through a variety of coping mechanisms.[220] In contrast, other studies have highlighted that life-threatening situations, violence, and profound losses can elevate

---

[217] Punamäki, 2009.

[218] Masten & Coatsworth, 1998; Masten, Powell, & Luthar, 2003; Werner, 1993.

[219] Masten & Coatsworth, 1998; Masten, Powell, & Luthar, 2003; Werner, 1993.

[220] Folkman, Lazarus, Gruen, and DeLongis, 1986.

psychological distress levels. Nevertheless, an intricate interplay of factors, encompassing the child, family, and broader societal context, in conjunction with psycho-socio-physiological processes, plays a pivotal role in safeguarding child development and mental health.[221]

It is essential to acknowledge that children inadvertently absorb a wide spectrum of information from their environment. Therefore, nurturing relationships with loving parents, positive peer interactions, and a supportive social network are indispensable for a child's development of effective coping strategies. While exposure to war and violence undoubtedly induces distress in children, societal, familial, and developmental considerations emerge as indispensable factors in the cultivation of resilience among these war-affected children. However, it remains imperative to underscore that the responsibility for resolving the underlying conflicts and political tensions leading to war should not rest upon the shoulders of the children, but rather on those of responsible adults through diplomatic and political means.[222]

Palestinians continue to survive and to stand together against political oppression and for their rights. At the same time, they must deal with soul-draining loss of loved ones, life-changing injuries, lasting medical conditions, destruction of homes, and a gloomy outlook for the future. How do they do it? Um Fadi and her family try to adapt to the changes, but face dire circumstances in any direction they turn:

> I have four daughters, ages 20 and under, and four sons, 25 and under. We had decided that we did not want to get into any arguments with anyone. So, we built a fence to serve as a wall around the piece of land we had purchased and covered it with a metal roof. Inside, I used a piece of cloth to serve as a wall, to separate my daughters and me from the boys and their father. We could not sleep at night. I swear to God. If you want, you can come and see how we live.

---

[221] Qouta, Punamäki, and El Sarraj, 2008, p. 310.

[222] Qouta, Punamäki, & El Sarraj, 2008.

When winter comes, we use an awning to protect us, but it gets filled with water, and starts to drip inside the house. I wake up the girls from their sleep. We are not safe from the mice, cockroaches, or the summer heat. What can I say, but to thank the Lord for everything. When we moved here it was a tragedy. The bread we ate was filled with sand. The dough had sand, the food had sand, even the bed we slept in. The sand was overwhelming, but at least now I put down a piece of plastic, and spread a mat on top, so we can eat a clean bite.

> However, thanks be to Allah, Allah gave me patience, and I hope to surround my children by good people. Each human feels sad, and Allah would provide him/her with patience. Allah is very generous as Allah provides people with patience and that's what happened to me. During the war, I saw many things no one else saw; however, thanks be to Allah. Thanks be to Allah that Allah compensated me with land. I hope that Allah would send me good people to build a house for me and my children there and get rid of the problems.

> When I walk with my daughter, throughout the length of the road I keep remembering the Lord. My daughter might ask me how I could say I feel that way. I would tell her, may the Lord punish those responsible for destroying our life.

> I am living in fear and horror. I am always praying to the Lord, to give my son good income so we can buy a piece of land in a safe area.

A conversation between a Palestinian mother and her war-traumatized daughter sheds some light on their state of mind as they try to deal with the threat of more war and violence on a daily basis.

Mother: "Dema, where did you just come from now?"

Dema: "From the club."

Mother: "Good girl, what did you do there? Who did you play with? With the other kids?

Dema: "Yes."

Mother: "Who destroyed our house that was here?"

Dema: "The Israelis."

Mother: "How many floors were in our house?"

Dema raises three fingers.

Mother: "When you grow up, which school do you want to attend, the one sponsored by the UNRWA or the government?"

Dema: "The UNRWA."

Mother: "Why is the UNRWA a better school? Is it because the education it provides is better? Well, OK. OK, my daughter, may you grow up, and may our home get rebuilt and become the way it used to be, so your brother can get married, and so I can buy you a beautiful dress to wear, and you will be happy. Say God willing, Amen, O Lord grant us that...Two wars, oh, we lived through two wars, and then where did we stay? In the house, where we stayed when the Israelis invaded us?"

Dema: "In the house."

Mother: "How did we escape, who gave us a ride to escape?"

Dima: "The ambulances."

Mother: "When was the invasion?"

Dima: "On Suhoor (a time when Muslims stop eating during Ramadan)."

Mother: "We were calling for help from the time we broke the fast, until the next day to hold the fast, until the ambulance came and helped us flee. What was the name of the guy they (Israelis) shot and killed?"

Dema: "Uncle."

Mother: "Uncle, whom?"

Dema: "Uncle Hossam."

Mother: "And who else?"

Dema and her Mother: "Saeed."

Mother: "They bombed the house while they were eating their breakfast.

"Do we like Israelis?"

Dema: "We don't like them."

Mother: "Why? What did they do to us?"

Dema: "The war."

There are psychological and pedagogical advantages to the process of parents instructing their children in the recollection and articulation of the events of war. This process is oftentimes culturally embedded, and within Palestinian familial discourse, the contemplation of warfare, including the veneration of the deceased, functions as psychological solace. These dialogues, founded on oral heritage, serve not only for the preservation of the collective psyche but also for the bequeathal of historical and cultural knowledge.[223]

In the realm of memory preservation, historical precedent points us to the aftermath of World War II. In nations profoundly marred by conflict such as Germany, France, and the United Kingdom, parents often passed on personal wartime narratives to the next generations. These conversations did not merely dwell on the gruesome events of war; they also highlighted personal sacrifices experienced or witnessed by the narrator, which cemented the legacy of the war's remembrances.[224] Similarly, Palestinian families invoke the power of oral tradition to perpetuate narratives. This art of storytelling, akin to an act of resistance, has been meticulously scrutinized by scholars like Edward Said, spotlighting the pivotal role of narratives in countering oppression while asserting Palestinian cultural identity and illuminating the triumph of resilience and defiance against occupation.[225]

Psychological research underscores the therapeutic merit inherent in the discourse surrounding traumatic experiences; it serves as a conduit for the emotive catharsis and the retroactive comprehension of one's history. When parents undertake these dialogues with their children, they not only impart personal sentiments and ordeals but also furnish a therapeutic channel for their own traumas.[226] Engaging in conversations about war and the solemn recognition of those who have departed allows for a cathartic process for both parents and children. The discipline of

---

[223] Fuchs, & Thelen, 2008.

[224] Kaminer, Stein, & Kleinman, 2000.

[225] Said, 984.

[226] Danieli, 1998.

psychology underscores the benefits of narrative exchange, particularly in the aftermath of traumatic episodes. By openly disseminating their experiences and confronting loss, families mutually partake in grieving, ultimately coming to terms with their collective anguish and constructing foundations of resilience.[227]

These familial dialogues support the vitality of the Palestinian people's collective consciousness as they resonate with personal testimonies, historical chronicles, and tales of fortitude. This example resonates with literature devoted to the intersections of conflict and memory, as elucidated by Jan Assmann's contributions to cultural memory theory. Assmann underscores the pivotal import of intergenerational transference of recollections as the foundation of identity and collective awareness.[228]

In the sphere of pedagogy, parents, through narratives of war, instill in their offspring the virtues of empathy, tolerance, and the imperativeness of peace.[229] These dialogues, concurrently, discharge the responsibility of instructing children in their history and the struggle for justice. This pedagogical ethos converges harmoniously with the tenets of Paulo Freire's "conscientization" or critical consciousness, which exalts the significance of dialogic engagement in the cultivation of a critical appreciation of one's historical and societal context.[230]

In the realm of communal and social sustenance, these conversations germinate a sense of kinship and support. Families, neighbors, and confidants convene to immortalize the memories of the departed and exchange narratives of their own experiences. This communal facet of storytelling is amply documented within the scholarship concerning collective responses to trauma and bereavement.[231]

Furthermore, these dialogues provide an avenue for parents to communicate a sense of continuity and stability for their families. By

---

[227] Neimeyer, 2003.

[228] Assmann, 2011.

[229] Winter, 2009.

[230] Freire, 1970.

[231] Kaniasty, & Norris, 2008.

highlighting the lessons learned from historical warfare, parents attempt to equip their children with the resolve to confront the unforeseen challenges of the future. The dialogues within Palestinian households, concerning war and the commemoration of the deceased, are steeped in the mission of safeguarding collective memory, negotiating the labyrinth of trauma, and transmitting cultural and historical knowledge. In so doing, these conversations construct both solace for individuals and fortitude for the Palestinian community, forging a path through the realities of adversity.

Clinical Implications

The outcomes of this study bear significant implications for mental health services and professionals engaged in aiding individuals exposed to the harrowing effects of war trauma, violence, and aggression. It is important to recognize that war trauma and violence cast a pervasive shadow over every stratum of society, exacting a particularly heavy toll on the most vulnerable and marginalized members—children.

Historically, interventions and therapeutic endeavors have predominantly centered on children directly impacted by the ravages of war. However, our research underscores the critical necessity for clinicians to delve into the experiences of both direct and indirect war trauma in their patients, highlighting the profound impact of these early life events on their development.

Children exposed to violence in their formative years exhibit marked disruptions in their early childhood development and parent-child relationships. These disruptions often culminate in subsequent attachment disturbances, characterized by diminished parental attunement, feelings of abandonment, and erratic home environments.[232] Moreover, early encounters with war trauma frequently precipitate anomalies or impairments in the regulation of metabolic, physiological, and psychological processes, alongside challenges in forming and sustaining interpersonal relationships

---

[232] Briere & Jordan, 2009; Shweder & Bourne, 1982.

and identity formation. These issues frequently manifest as mental health problems persisting into adulthood.[233]

The child exposed to war violence may internalize aspects of the trauma, giving rise to distorted perceptions of self and others and the cultivation of maladaptive worldviews. In this context, clinicians must employ therapeutic strategies[234] to tackle the range of challenges arising from clients' internal emotional states, which in turn influence their outward behavior and symptomatic presentations.

Therapists should be equipped to address avoidance-type behaviors such as substance abuse, dissociation, and suicidality, while facilitating healthier coping mechanisms for emotional distress rooted in war trauma. A pivotal goal of treatment involves collaborative efforts between therapist and patient to reconfigure outdated interpersonal schemas that no longer serve a purpose in nonviolent contexts. Concurrently, therapy aids clients in developing more accurate perspectives on their worldview, self-perception, and relationships, ultimately ameliorating symptoms associated with war trauma-induced psychopathologies such as anxiety, depression, and PTSD.

The intricate nature of war trauma necessitates clinicians' adeptness in diverse theoretical approaches and the ability to work with integrative methodology. These facets are indispensable for the effective treatment of this population. Therapists must not only cultivate an awareness of vicarious traumatization but also deeply comprehend the ramifications of war trauma on children's lives and mental well-being. Failure to recognize and validate a client's war trauma experiences can impede the therapeutic process, potentially leading to the reenactment of traumatic episodes, yielding anxiety, fear, and re-traumatization.

Our study's findings furnish valuable contributions to clinical assessments and treatment planning. They shed light on the profound impact of war trauma on child development, parent-child relationships, family dynamics, and the potential for re-traumatization. By considering

---

[233] Pearlman & Courtois, 2005; Stovall-McClough & Cloitre, 2006; Allen, 2008; Briere, Hodges, & Godbout, 2010; Hooven, Nurius, Logan-Greene, & Thompson, 2012; Springer, Sheridan, Kuo, & Carnes, 2007.

[234] Cloitre, Cohen, & Scarvalone, 2002.

these factors, clinicians can enhance their case conceptualizations, providing a more comprehensive understanding of the range of war trauma experiences and family dynamics that may affect a client's present-day functioning and well-being.

To facilitate the therapeutic alliance and the healing journey, therapists must explore various facets of clients' subjective experiences within a persistently war-torn environment. The therapeutic setting should serve as a secure and efficacious space wherein children who have endured war trauma can delve into their historical trauma-related experiences and reflect upon the impact of these experiences on their lives. It is imperative for therapists to provide a nurturing environment where the voices of war-affected children can be heard, validated, and comprehended. Clinicians and service providers must also acknowledge and honor the emotions, thoughts, and experiences of war-affected children. Consequently, the therapeutic environment becomes a powerful tool for these children to openly share and process their experiences.

Our research underscores the imperative of broadening the spectrum of family therapy interventions when dealing with patients hailing from war-ravaged environments. Mental health professionals and service providers must recognize that direct and indirect war trauma affects each family member differently. Therefore, it is essential to assess the psychosocial effects, support mechanisms, coping strategies, and relational dynamics of each family member to gain a comprehensive understanding of the impact of war on the family system. Such an approach enables clinicians to explore clients' coping styles and familial relationships more deeply.

Efforts dedicated to the study and support of children and adolescents affected by the profound ramifications of war can significantly advance through the adoption of integrative methodologies. These approaches should encompass a comprehensive examination of the multifaceted factors contributing to aggression, incorporating the intricate interplay of individual, familial, and societal influences. By embracing such holistic perspectives, we can foster a more empathetic and comprehensive understanding of the challenges faced by these young individuals, ultimately guiding more effective interventions and support mechanisms to help them navigate the adversities they encounter. Psychological interventions for these traumatized children should commence early in their development, as the cognitive-emotional processes that underlie aggression risks are intricately linked to their social experiences and neurophysiological maturation.[235] Moreover, interventions should be sensitive to developmental stages and comprehensively address deficiencies in psychophysiological, cognitive, and emotional processing of war experiences.

Our study also reveals valuable insights into coping strategies, family dynamics, and resilience. Clinicians can leverage the coping mechanisms of clients' families to navigate recurring relational themes, shedding light on how clients reenact war trauma and problematic social dynamics in their peer and societal interactions. Additionally, clinicians should identify and explore clients' reflective coping and resiliency strategies tied to their war experiences.

Our study underscores the urgent need for concerted efforts to support war-affected children and their families grappling with psychological and emotional challenges. Systematic intervention programs must be devised to disrupt the transgenerational transmission of war trauma. One potential avenue is to equip children with the tools to recognize emotional states, fostering more adaptive responses to trauma. Such initiatives have the potential to enhance prosocial development, underpinning both individual flourishing and societal harmony.

Furthermore, it is essential to tailor interventions to the cultural and social context in which these children reside. Western-centric individual therapy approaches may prove less effective in Eastern cultures, where community involvement and family integration are paramount. Thus, clinicians must be attuned to the cultural nuances of healing and fostering recovery at both individual and societal levels.

Ultimately, the reconstruction of societies torn apart by war, encompassing social and economic networks, cultural institutions, and the fundamental respect for human rights, stands as a cornerstone of healing. Above all, it is incumbent upon us to work towards the cessation of all wars, ensuring that future generations are spared the ravages of psychological trauma and devastation.

---

[235] Yule, 2002.

CONCLUSION:

"We need the international community to start caring about Palestinian children who are the future of our society"

Human behavior is a complex interplay of individual and environmental factors. The individual element encompasses a person's unique characteristics, desires, values, attitudes, and personal traits, all shaped by psychological composition. Conversely, the environmental component encapsulates the external conditions that surround and influence an individual. The dynamic interaction between these two dimensions molds a person's development as they progress through different life stages.

Palestinian children, like their counterparts worldwide, undergo profound influences from their environment, genetic inheritance, societal circumstances, and the prevailing culture within their family, school, and country. These multifaceted elements invariably manifest in the behavior, responses, emotional states, and personality development of these children. The field of mental health has made significant strides in scrutinizing the factors and experiences that mold human personality. Thus, my study sought to delve into how Israeli wars and aggression against Palestinian children impact their mental health and psychological well-being.

Wars are an unfortunate global reality, and the aftermath of these conflicts has drawn the attention of researchers, particularly concerning the trauma experienced by children since World War II.[236] The literature surveyed in this work encompasses studies conducted worldwide, highlighting the various adversities faced by children as a direct or indirect consequence of exposure to war-related experiences. These investigations

---

[236] Jensen, 1993.

consistently illustrate the high prevalence of psychological effects on children, which often persist alongside physical injuries. A notable focus lies in understanding the enduring repercussions of such trauma, with several follow-up studies demonstrating its profound and enduring impact on children's mental health. The diagnostic criteria for post-traumatic stress disorder (PTSD) in children have evolved, underscoring the veracity of PTSD as a diagnosis arising from war-related trauma.

Many studies underscore the distinctive manifestations of war trauma in children, influenced by their respective countries. Some studies indicate that war trauma in children may take on different forms, depending upon the country of the child.[237] In the Palestinian context, the entire nation grapples with marginalization on the global stage, adding an extra layer of trauma.[238] Some children face displacement from their homeland to refugee camps, while others are exposed to the war's immediacy, constantly witnessing its ravages. Despite these contextual differences, common themes emerge in children's responses to traumatic or life-threatening events, including somatization, withdrawal symptoms, posttraumatic disorders, anxiety, unresolved grief, excessive fear, sleep disturbances, bedwetting, increased attachment to parents, and developmental regression. These reactions can evolve into enduring mental health conditions, necessitating professional intervention.

These critical issues persist among Palestinian children, with the psychological damage often left unaddressed by both the psychological community and influential political actors. Consequently, these issues fester and persist as a chronic affliction in their lives. Regrettably, Palestinian children have grown accustomed to these challenges and are even queried about their feelings concerning them in educational settings. Surprisingly, 66% of Palestinian children opt to focus their educational efforts on the issue of war, while 24.7% contemplate martyrdom, with boys more inclined toward this option (67.8%) than girls (32.2%). A smaller

---

[237] Albertyn, Bickler, Van As, Millar, & Rode, 2003; Angel, Hjern, & Ingleby, 2001; Lasser & Adams, 2007; Leavitt & Fox, 2014; Zahr, 1996.

[238] Qouta et al., 1995b; Qouta et al., 1997; Qouta & El Sarraj, 2004; Rought-Brooks, 2015.

percentage (8.7%) advocates for the peace process, while an even smaller fraction (0.1%) expresses willingness to participate in a national struggle, and 0.5% prioritize religious piety.

The suffering endured by Palestinian children through intermittent hostilities and open warfare spanning six decades has cast a somber shadow. Extensive research attests to the psychological afflictions these children endure, underscoring the emergence of a protracted mental health crisis. The breakdown of families, loss of homes and neighborhoods, and the pervasive fear experienced represent only a fraction of the mounting predicament. Through the lens of the children, the entire Palestinian nation has become a society deeply scarred by constant, repetitive trauma.

The present study specifically investigated the impact of Israeli war and aggression on the Gaza Strip in 2014 on Palestinian children and their family members, who were directly targeted by Israeli forces. The study's findings unequivocally point to the profound emotional and psychological suffering experienced by children exposed to the horrors of war, resulting in a spectrum of mental health problems. However, amidst the harrowing circumstances, the research also unearthed varying coping mechanisms. Some children resorted to rationalization and avoidance as defense mechanisms against the psychological trauma, while others relied on denial, problem-solving, family support, external sources of stability, and prosocial interactions through family, peers, or society. Moreover, adaptive coping strategies emerged as resilient sources of strength, including a positive perception and deep regard for their homeland. These children displayed unwavering determination, viewing their plight as an integral part of their struggle for freedom, peace, and dignity. In summation, resilience shines as a beacon of hope among Palestinian children exposed to the ravages of war trauma.

In the Gaza Strip, the enduring cycle of war, violence, and devastation has inflicted profound and lasting suffering upon the entire society. A particularly poignant illustration of this anguish emerged during the 2014 Israeli military operation in the Gaza Strip, which wrought catastrophic consequences upon the vulnerable Palestinian children residing there. The harrowing ordeal, spanning 50 agonizing days, exacted a grievous toll, with an estimated 2,191 Palestinians losing their lives. Alarmingly, nearly 70% of these casualties were innocent civilians, including a heart-wrenching tally of 527 children.[239] The tragedy was compounded by the fact that at least 142 Palestinian families bore the unbearable burden of losing multiple family members during this period.[240]

An estimated 6,000 children now grapple with the lifelong burden of having a parent left permanently disabled as a result of the conflict. Additionally, approximately 1,000 children have been left with life-altering disabilities due to injuries sustained during the conflict. These numbers only begin to encapsulate the scale of suffering endured. The Palestinian Ministry of Health reported a staggering 11,100 Palestinians, of which 3,374 were children, sustained injuries during this tumultuous period.[241]

The destruction wrought upon the Gaza Strip was not confined to human lives alone. Over 16,000 housing units lay in ruins or suffered severe damage as a result of the Israeli bombings. This left nearly 118,000 people homeless, with an overwhelming majority being children who now found themselves without shelter, their lives upended in an instant. Furthermore, according to UNICEF, a staggering 373,000 children in Gaza were in desperate need of psychosocial support to help them grapple with the traumatic experiences they had endured.[242] Despite the valiant efforts of organizations such as UNICEF, the United Nations Relief and Works Agency for Palestine Refugees (UNRWA), and Community Mental Health Programme,[243] which provided essential counseling and support services, a significant number of children—nearly 330,000—remained without the psychosocial support they so urgently required.[244]

The grim reality is that these adversities have left an indelible mark on the mental and emotional well-being of Palestinian children. A striking

---

[239] PCHR, 2014.

[240] UN, 2014b.

[241] UN, 2014b.

[242] UNICEF, 2014.

[243] Rought-Brooks, 2015.

[244] UNICEF, 2014.

95% of Palestinian children now exhibit manifestations of mental health distress, including but not limited to depression, hyperactivity, a tendency to withdraw from social interaction, and heightened levels of aggression.[245] This study seeks to shed light on the profound physical, psychological, and life-altering ramifications of Israel's continuous wars on Palestinians living in the Gaza strip, with a focus on the Protective Edge military campaign in 2014 and a specific focus on the repercussions borne by the children of Gaza. This work sought to provide a platform for these children to share their lived experiences, while striving to comprehend the profound trauma they have endured.

Wa'd, whose home was bombed and totally destroyed, is still homeless with her family. She suffers from depression and became an introvert and socially withdrawn. She expressed her feelings:

> We are children and there is no place safe for us. I am getting tired just to hear the word "war." I am living in a place where I do not have safety and no comfort...all my dreams suddenly crumbled to ashes.

> They forced us to flee to Sinai, we felt we are pushed out of the whole country. We fled to the schools in Jabalia Camp and we shared the rooms with other families. We divided the rooms with a piece of cloth where men can sit outside and women inside. Twenty-four hours you have to wear your headscarf. If I needed to go to the bathroom, I have to take a companion with me. Psychologically, I was not comfortable living there. The place is not suitable to live in, but what can you say, this is our destiny.

Maysaa, who was severely injured and lost family members in a bombing, expresses her fears:

> When I remember what happened, I become obsessed with it. When I see someone on the street, I ask them, do you think the war is over? They would reply, there is a war coming that

---

[245] Al Jazeera, 2018.

is going to be worse than what we have already been through. I think to myself, are we better off than the ones who got killed?

I then think, we can manage because we are old enough, but what about the children, what will happen to them? How are we going to help the little ones escape and protect them? As I relate that, I can hear my little sister screaming and crying.

Drawings by Palestinian children detail the war machine that confronts them: Israeli soldiers, tanks, jets, drones. The depictions show the destruction of homes, friends, and family. The helplessness these children feel is manifest in these drawings. Dr. Qadih summarizes the psychological suffering of Palestinian children in Gaza:

The children of the 2014 war until now have not received any help from the international community, or other social care, largely because the international community does not give any attention to the Palestinian people's needs and suffering. The international community appears to view the impact as temporary; they see the physical injuries but not the emotional scars. The international community needs to see the impact of suffering on human emotions and passions, and their impact on future potential. The international community ignores the psychological needs and wounds of the Palestinian children.

I assure you that 90 to 95% of Palestinian children need comprehensive psychological care. Comprehensive psychological care does not come in a short period of time, it is not a short-term therapy lasting three to six months. Comprehensive psychological care requires long-term therapy lasting three to five years in order to restore the mental wellbeing of the children. All throughout my work with Palestinian children that visit our clinic, I found that these children suffer from behavioral, psychological, mental, and emotional disorders. With our limited resources we try to provide as much psychological support as we can to our clients, but it inevitably falls short.

In the Gaza Strip, we do not have the resources for mental health or the public to help the people. Mental health is not seen as an important issue despite the urgent need for it. The population in Gaza, young and old, needs psychological support or treatment. This is the beginning of the real treatment and the beginning of healing, but we have no support in this field. Our limited resources of few trained therapists are not enough to provide the specialized treatment and the services needed for these children to heal.

In fact, the resources we have are almost zero. There are some lights here and there that illuminate the way for the people, but it is not enough. Therefore, we are calling on the international community to stand with us by providing the resources to establish specialized clinics that can provide counseling and psychological services that war victims need, especially the children.

Secondly, we need better vocational training, to create psychotherapist specialists who have the training to relieve traumatic stress. When sick and suffering individuals look for services, they are expecting results. When a child, adolescent, or woman is suffering from psychological issues, they are searching for treatment and healing, and this should start to produce results quickly. This requires a high standard of training and professionalism.

In summary, we need to open specialized clinics, provide high-quality training, and be able to rely on supervisors to provide professional guidance for psychological counseling and treatment. These three aspects are crucial if the community is to heal and achieve long-lasting security, safety, and peace.

When others extend their hand to help a poor or orphan child, they are providing compassion and care to help them feel safe and secure. The same kind of support is also very much needed for a therapist, who must stay strong and resilient in the face of so much suffering. Therapists need the support to help deal with all the psychological diseases that overwhelm us all at once as a result of the especially tumultuous suffering associated with war. We need the international community to start caring about Palestinian children who are the future of our society.

Dr. Sami Owaida summed up the entire problematic situation by pointing to the only possible viable solution on the horizon. Dr. Owaida recognizes that Gaza is in a destructive cycle that creates many pressures that build continuously, which will not depressurize until a political solution emerges. He is forced to acknowledge the reality that medical and psychological remedies, no matter how effective, will only fall short until there is a political remedy:

> This is a natural result of the siege imposed on the Palestinian people, and it creates a compound trauma. In the last war many children lost their parents. Their father died, his mother or his brother or a loved one. This is also a complex shock. You live and you lose a friend, and you're not only emotionally shocked by the trauma itself, but that loss of someone dear to you becomes even greater with the added loss of a home that's been destroyed, so that even the loss of a children's game from playtime becomes hard to bear.
>
> I can tell you that it is difficult to predict what will happen because I think even politically that the increase in pressure generates an explosion, and this explosion will affect in one way or other parties that exert pressure on the Palestinian people. I do not want to talk about politics, but part of the psychological factors that frustrate the Palestinian people are the states of division. The division has distorted the Palestinian cause. Unfortunately, this is one of the pressure factors. It is the result of the political pressures and the result of the occupation.
>
> All these factors create an unhealthy situation psychologically. I do not expect any improvement at the psychological level or psychological programs without a political solution to the issue, because the issue is a political issue par excellence.

Dr. Owaida maintains a belief in the Palestinian people and looks forward to the day when they will be sympathized with enough to allow them the right and freedom to live normal, healthy lives. Until then, he remains amazed at their resilience.

Despite the difficulties experienced by the Palestinian people, the suffering—the frustration and the lack of a horizon for any solution—despite this, I'm impressed both internally and externally to witness how these people can stand and continue to live despite all the torments they receive every day. This indicates the strong determination and strong faith in the rights of the Palestinian people and their just cause that we want to reach the whole world.

I believe that the world has begun to deal with us on this basis because, before we are Palestinians or Muslims, we are human beings and we are entitled to live. Our children have the right to live freely, to live their childhood as all the children of the world.

This is a message through you to the whole free and civilized world, to all my colleagues in mental health and to all human beings, to practice the natural right as human beings to support our just Palestinian cause, and we demand no more than to regain our rights and to live free as we live in all countries of the world, except under the Israeli occupation.

I interviewed participants cited in this book during the years 2016 to 2021. As of September 2018, four years after the 2014 war, the Gaza Strip had been besieged by Israeli occupation for over a decade. Palestinians in the Gaza strip continue to suffer from the blockade imposed by Israeli and Egyptian governments since 2007, severely restricting the movement of people and goods and contributing to dire living conditions.

On March 30, 2018, a profound and resonant chapter in the Palestinian struggle for justice and self-determination unfolded along the Gaza border. This transformative movement, aptly christened the "Great March of Return," bore witness to the collective plea for the cessation of Israeli occupation blockade upon Gaza. The demonstrators further articulated their demand for the recognition of the right of Palestinian refugees and their descendants to return to their ancestral lands and sought to register their protest against the relocation of the United States Embassy from Tel Aviv to Jerusalem. Regrettably, the demands of these demonstrators were met with a tragic eruption of violence, as the Israeli military responded with disproportionate and lethal force. Tear gas and live ammunition were indiscriminately deployed, resulting in the tragic loss of over 150 Palestinian lives, while approximately 10,000 individuals sustained grievous injuries. Among these casualties, Robert Mardini, who held the esteemed position of Regional Director for the Near and Middle East for the International Committee of the Red Cross (ICRC) from 2012 to 2018, conveyed the distressing fact that a significant portion, approximately 1,400 individuals, sustained multiple gunshot wounds, of three to five bullets each.[246]

Another tragic episode, "Operation Guardian of the Walls," began on May 10th, 2021, and persisted until May 21st, 2021. This 11-day war was borne of the simmering tensions surrounding the potential eviction of Palestinian families from the Sheikh Jarrah neighborhood in East Jerusalem. The attack was further fueled by clashes that erupted at the Al-Aqsa Mosque compound during the sacred month of Ramadan. Marked by relentless bombardments by Israeli forces upon the Gaza Strip, the consequences were heartrending. The conflict exacted an egregious loss of life and the widespread ruination of vital infrastructure, causing a staggering 261 Gazan deaths, among them 67 children and 41 women, and over 2,200 individuals were injured. The conflict also precipitated the internal displacement of more than 113,000 Palestinians, including 685 children and 480 women, many of whom sought refuge in UNRWA schools. Regrettably, over 1,770 housing units were either obliterated or heavily damaged. Beyond this physical devastation, crucial civilian infrastructure, including residences, educational institutions, medical facilities, and water and sanitation systems, suffered extensive harm. And

---

[246] AFP & TOI Staff, 2018.

of course, the psychological trauma inflicted upon civilians, particularly children, was profound and enduring.[247]

The conflict continued on May 9th, 2023, when Israeli fighter jets once more unleashed their fury upon the Gaza Strip, a campaign christened "Operation Shield and Arrow." This offensive followed a large-scale Israeli military operation in Jenin, within the confines of the occupied West Bank, and lasted until May 13th. The Israeli attacks claimed the lives of 11 Palestinian civilians, including four innocent children. According to the Ministry of Health in Gaza, a total of 190 individuals were left wounded, of whom 64 were young children. The Israeli military operations also damaged 2,943 housing units, including the complete obliteration of 103 homes. The resulting displacement crisis included at least 1,244 Palestinians who were forced to seek new shelter, according to the Palestinian Ministry of Public Works. [248]

Israel Israeli occupation persists in employing psychological warfare strategies designed to induce mental and emotional distress within the Palestinian population. These tactics encompass the continual presence of drones, the deployment of snipers, with the specific aim of targeting Palestinian individuals, and periodic bombings—all culminating in the creation of an atmosphere characterized by fear and instability.

Amnesty International, in its pursuit of truth and justice, undertook a meticulous investigation of nine Israeli airstrikes, scrutinizing their impact on civilians and the consequential damage and destruction of residential edifices in the Gaza Strip. Their report revealed a disconcerting pattern: The attacks "were launched into densely populated urban areas at 2am when families were sleeping at home, which suggests that those who planned and authorized the attacks anticipated—and likely disregarded—the disproportionate harm to civilians. Intentionally launching disproportionate attacks, a pattern Amnesty International has documented in previous Israeli operations, is a war crime."[249]

---

[247] Al Jazeera, 2022.

[248] Israel/OPT: Civilian Deaths and Extensive Destruction in Latest Gaza Offensive Highlight Human Toll of Apartheid, 2023

[249] Amnesty International, 2023

2023-2024 War

On the 7th of October 2023, an armed conflict erupted between Israeli occupation and the Palestinians in the Gaza Strip once again. Subsequently, Israeli forces initiated an extensive aerial bombardment campaign on Gaza, followed by a large-scale ground invasion. As of February 10th, 2024, more than 28,064 Palestinians, 70% of them are children and women who have lost their lives due to continuous Israeli attacks on the Gaza Strip, according to statements from Palestinian health officials. There is no indication of a ceasefire in the besieged enclave. [250]

The number of individuals wounded since the commencement of the bombardment has climbed to 67,611, as reported by a spokesperson from the Health Ministry.[251] Numerous Palestinian victims remain trapped beneath the rubble, aggravated by an Israeli siege, restricting access to essential goods such as fuel, food, and electricity. The total count of Palestinian casualties is anticipated to rise. The substantial casualties can be attributed to Israeli occupation indiscriminate bombardment targeting civilian residences, hospitals, refugee camps, mosques, churches, and schools. Residents in the Gaza Strip are left without shelter, without food, without drink, without medicine, and without protection.

---

[250] وزارة الصحة الفلسطينية (**Palestinian Health Ministry**), n.d.

[251] وزارة الصحة الفلسطينية (**Palestinian Health Ministry**), n.d.

Table 7

PALESTINIAN CHILDREN KILLED AND INJURED BY ISRAELI FORCES UP TO FEBRUARY 10TH, 2024 DURING THE ISRAELI WAR ON THE GAZA STRIP

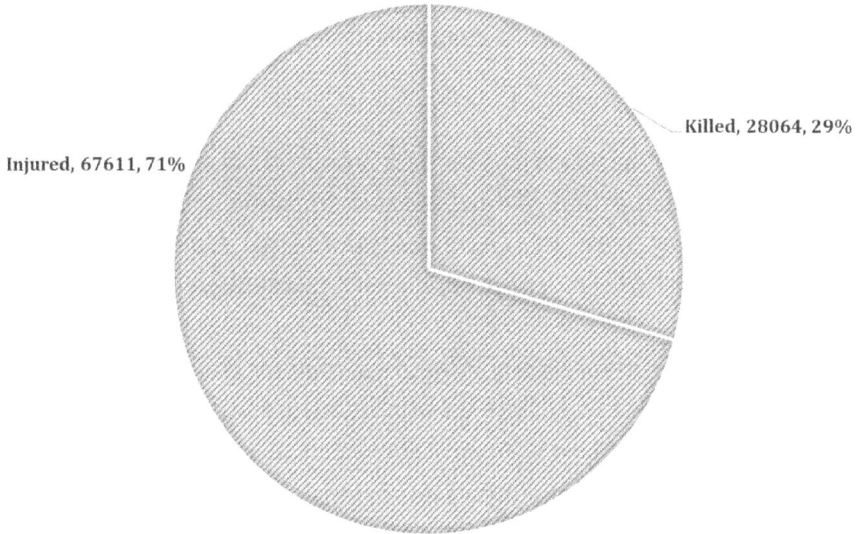

Killed, 28064, 29%

Injured, 67611, 71%

Source:

وزارة الصحة الفلسطينية

(Palestinian Health Ministry). (n.d.). Telegram.
Retrieved February 10th, 2024, from https://t.me/MOHMediaGaza

Despite international calls for a ceasefire, the Israeli occupation and its primary ally, the United States, have dismissed such appeals, contending that halting the hostilities would provide Hamas an opportunity to regroup. Fikr Shalltoot, Medical Aid for Palestinians (MAP), a United Kingdom-based organization's Gaza director asked, "How many more deaths will it take for this assault to be brought to an end – 50,000, 100,000?...As we witness our homes, hospitals and schools turned to rubble, we are crying out for a shred of humanity from world leaders." [252] "Are you enjoying this…horror movie?" Zak Hania, a resident of the al-Shati refugee camp, asked world leaders in an interview with Al Jazeera. [253] "How many people need to die, to be killed, for the people, for the world, for the world leaders to move to do something? We asked for a ceasefire. We are all civilians." [254]

During our interview, Dr. Sami Owaida, (as mentioned earlier, a psychiatric consultant for children and adolescents from the Gaza Community Mental Health Programme), described the current situation in Gaza:

How could the war end if the Gaza Strip is still besieged by air, land, and sea? You are in prison. We are besieged, in prison and occupied, and the simplest types of freedoms have been confiscated. Until a person lives in dignity, we are still under pressure, which takes different forms.

There is no doubt for any Palestinian, even the child, that the Israeli occupation continues to practice the utmost torture against the Palestinian people through the impoverishment of the Palestinian people, and through lack of assistance obtaining important materials for industry and trade.

Clearly, there is still no end in sight to the murder and turmoil.

Afterword

Children residing in conflict-ridden regions worldwide grapple with profound psychological repercussions stemming from their exposure to the harrowing consequences of warfare. Among these vulnerable children, one finds both Palestinian and Israeli youth, who bear enduring emotional scars wrought by the protracted conflict in the region. This enduring and

252 More than 10,000 Palestinians Killed in Israeli Attacks on Gaza, n.d.

253 More than 10,000 Palestinians Killed in Israeli Attacks on Gaza, n.d.

254 More than 10,000 Palestinians Killed in Israeli Attacks on Gaza, n.d.

agonizing discord between Palestinians and Israelis persists as a painful, relentless, and chronic reality.

A cursory examination of pertinent literature and lived experiences underscores the imperative for intensified efforts in comprehending the intricate web of psychological repercussions faced by Palestinian children residing in the Gaza Strip, a demographic profoundly affected by protracted exposure to the ravages of war and violence. A proactive approach is warranted, entailing the development of comprehensive programs aimed at affording these young individuals the tools necessary for psychological resilience and well-being. Furthermore, advocating for the safeguarding of their psychological welfare is an ethical imperative of the utmost urgency.

The overarching goal should be twofold: first, to terminate the suffering and trauma, and second, to alleviate the anguish endured by Palestinian children. The cyclical pattern of war and violence must be disrupted, making way for the restoration and reverence of human dignity and rights. It is essential to acknowledge that, among the victims of Israeli measures—such as house bombings, attacks on schools and hospitals, protracted sieges, loss of life, and physical and emotional devastation—the youngest members of the Gaza community bear the brunt of the suffering.

Regrettably, as witnessed during my recent visits to Gaza, these children also bear the heavy burden of shattered innocence, bereft of the sanctuary to fully embrace their childhood. They are left emotionally traumatized and robbed of the simple joys of childhood. Thus, the collective conscience of humanity beckons us to transcend the status quo, recognizing that we possess the capacity to effect positive change and, in so doing, rekindle hope for a future where the innocence and well-being of all children, regardless of their origin, can be safeguarded with compassion and empathy.

APPENDIX A:

Destruction, Killing, Physical Injuries, Emotional and Psychological Effects of the Israeli Wars on Palestinian Children in Photos

in the Gaza Strip during 2014 Israeli war on Gaza

Israeli destruction to Palestinian homes in the Gaza Strip during 2014 Israeli war on Gaza

Israeli destruction to Palestinian homes in the Gaza Strip during 2014 Israeli war on Gaza

Israeli destruction to Palestinian homes in the Gaza Strip during 2014 Israeli war on Gaza

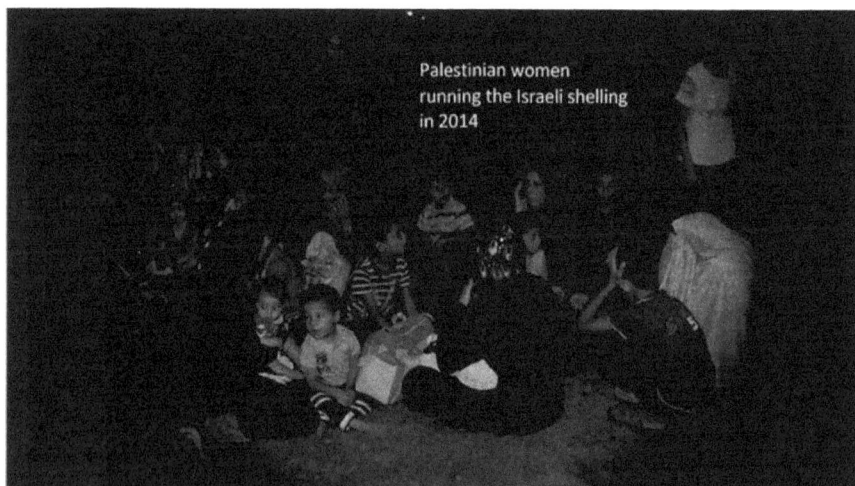

Palestinian women running the Israeli shelling in 2014

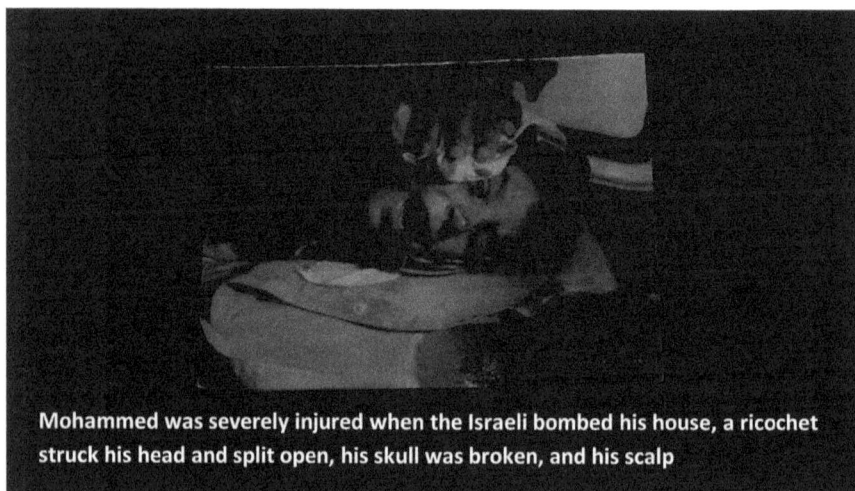

Mohammed was severely injured when the Israeli bombed his house, a ricochet struck his head and split open, his skull was broken, and his scalp

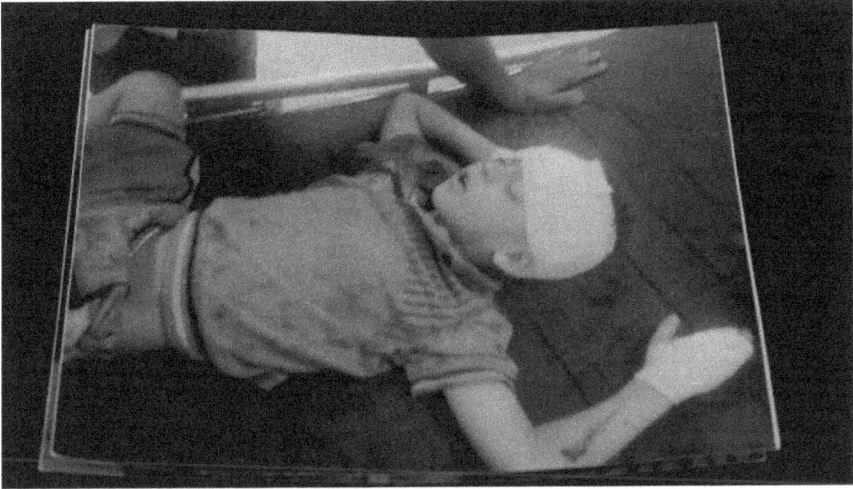

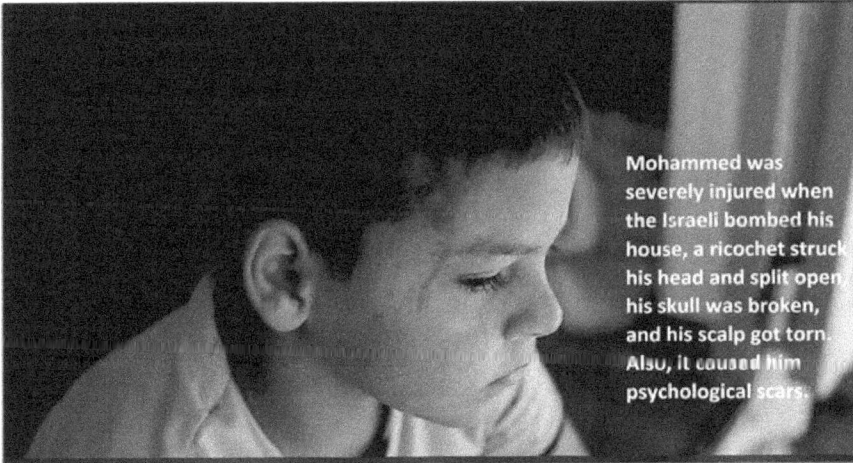

Mohammed was severely injured when the Israeli bombed his house, a ricochet struck his head and split open, his skull was broken, and his scalp got torn. Also, it caused him psychological scars.

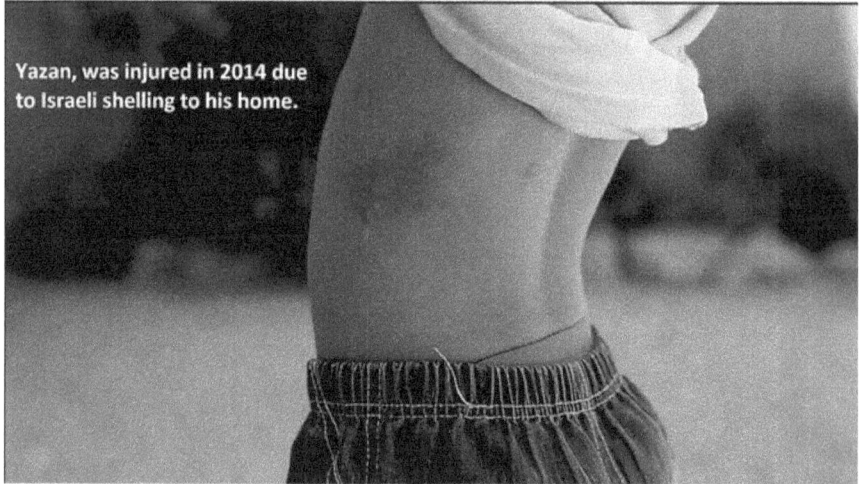

Yazan, was injured in 2014 due to Israeli shelling to his home.

The Wahdan family lost their mother was killed, the father legs were amputated, and the three children were seriously injured. 12 family members were killed by the Israeli bombing on the family including granddad, grandmother, uncle, 2 of his kids, they were 12 and 14 years old. 2 young daughters, the nieces, a little child age 2years old, and a little child age 4-year-old were killed as well

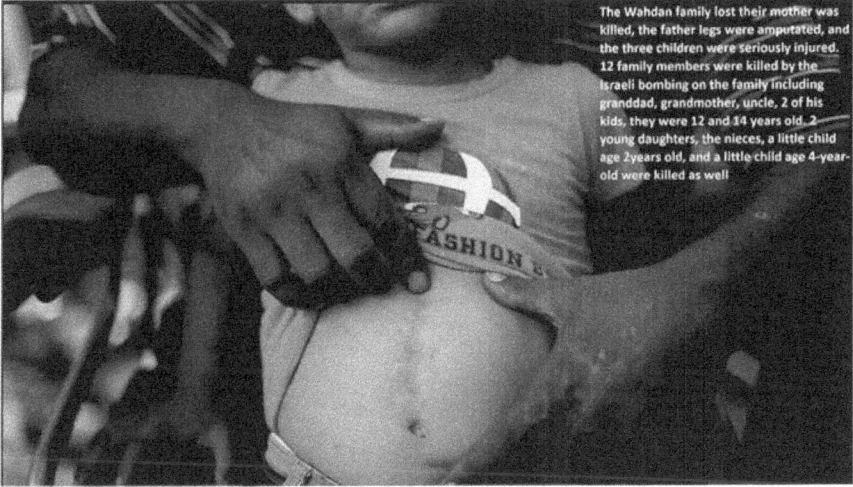

The Wahdan family lost their mother was killed, the father legs were amputated, and the three children were seriously injured. 12 family members were killed by the Israeli bombing on the family including granddad, grandmother, uncle, 2 of his kids, they were 12 and 14 years old, 2 young daughters, the nieces, a little child age 2years old, and a little child age 4-year-old were killed as well

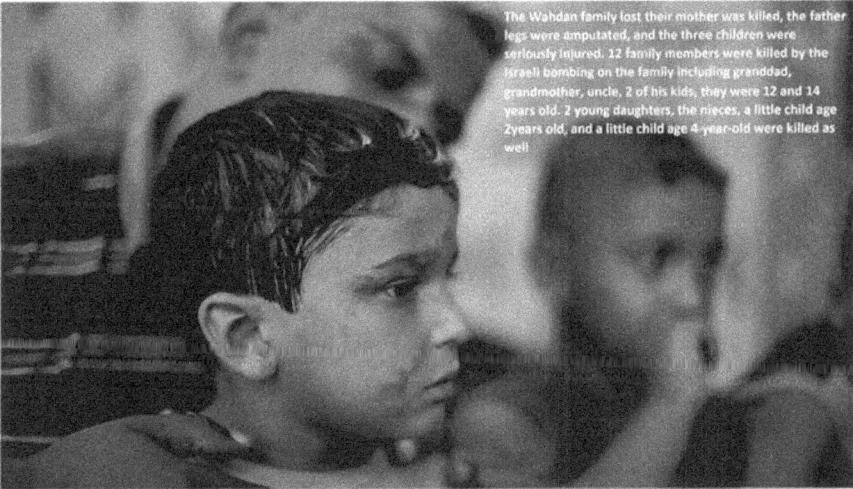

The Wahdan family lost their mother was killed, the father legs were amputated, and the three children were seriously injured. 12 family members were killed by the Israeli bombing on the family including granddad, grandmother, uncle, 2 of his kids, they were 12 and 14 years old. 2 young daughters, the nieces, a little child age 2years old, and a little child age 4-year-old were killed as well

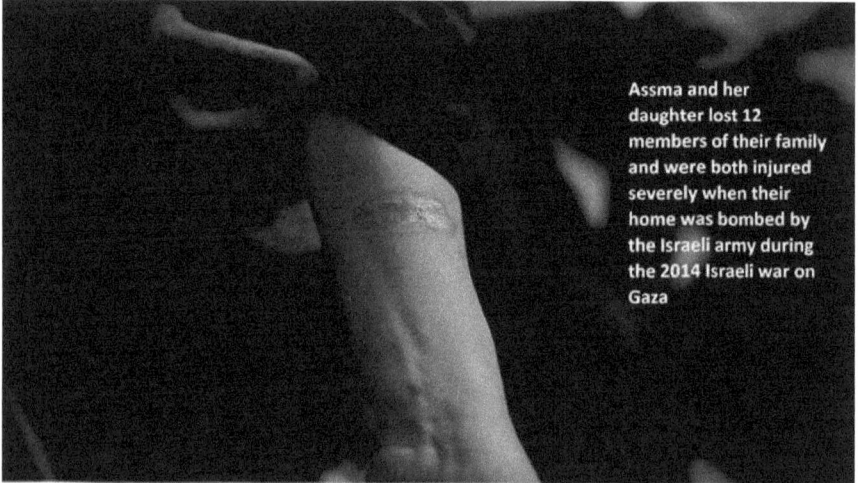

Assma and her daughter lost 12 members of their family and were both injured severely when their home was bombed by the Israeli army during the 2014 Israeli war on Gaza

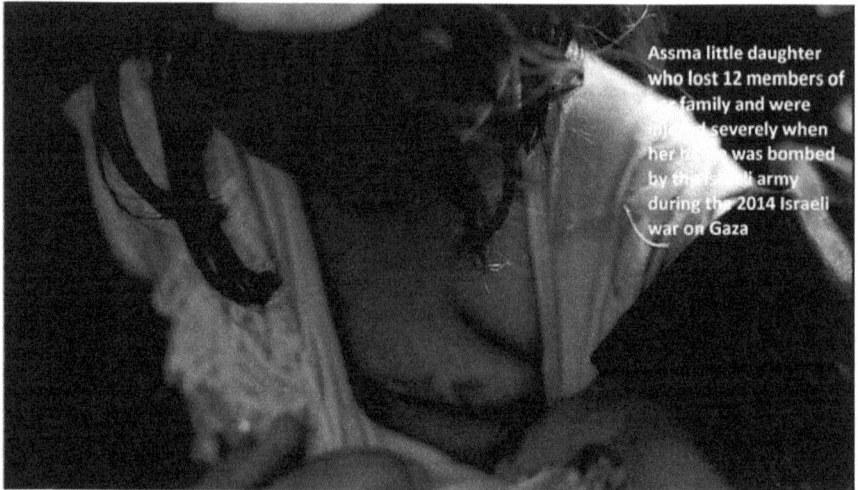

Assma little daughter who lost 12 members of family and were injured severely when her home was bombed by the Israeli army during the 2014 Israeli war on Gaza

Umm Salah home was hit by an Israeli missile while they were home. Her three children, husband, and self were injured. Her oldest son, Moayad, body was buried except his face after the missile landed on their home. Moayad suffered from internal bleeding in his stomach. Her daughter, Ghada, was injured in the stomach. Her other son, Hamuda was injured in his face and head from the missile shrapnel's. She was injured in the foot.

The homes Palestinians families live currently after the Israeli army bombed their homes in 2014 war

Dema family trailer which was given to them to live in after their house was bombed by the Israelis during the 2014 war

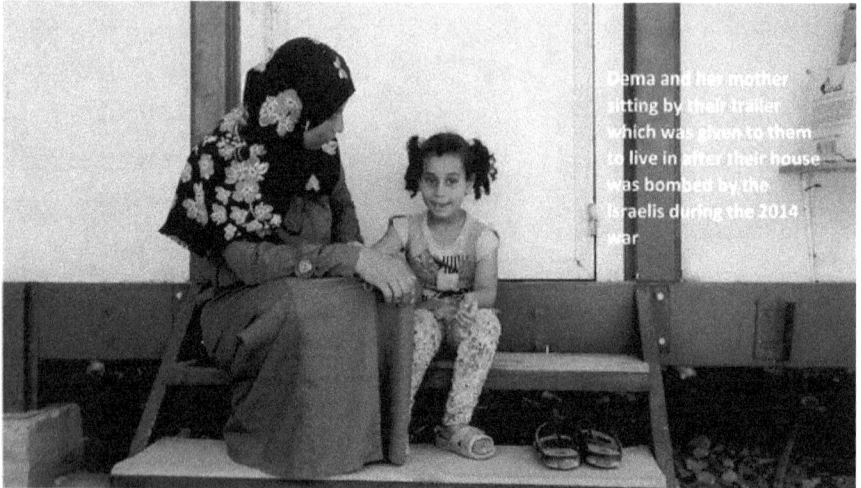

Dema and her mother sitting by their trailer which was given to them to live in after their house was bombed by the Israelis during the 2014 war

Umm Fadi living condition after the Israeli bombed her house

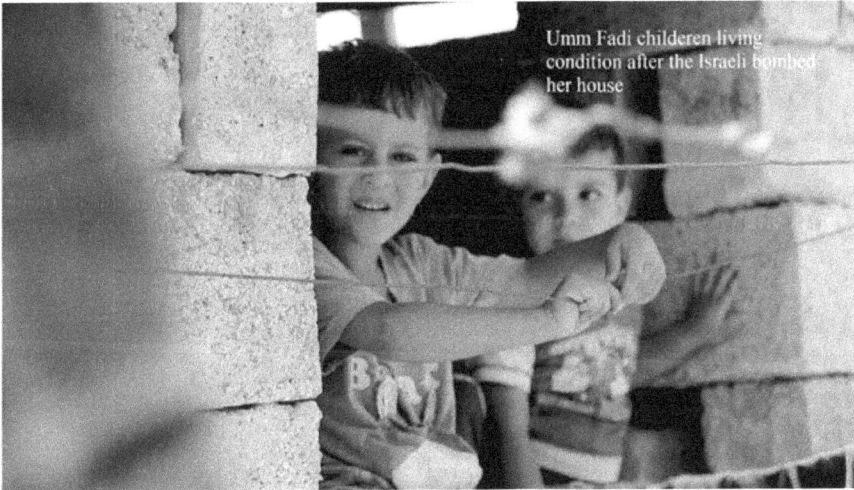

Umm Fadi childeren living condition after the Israeli bombed her house

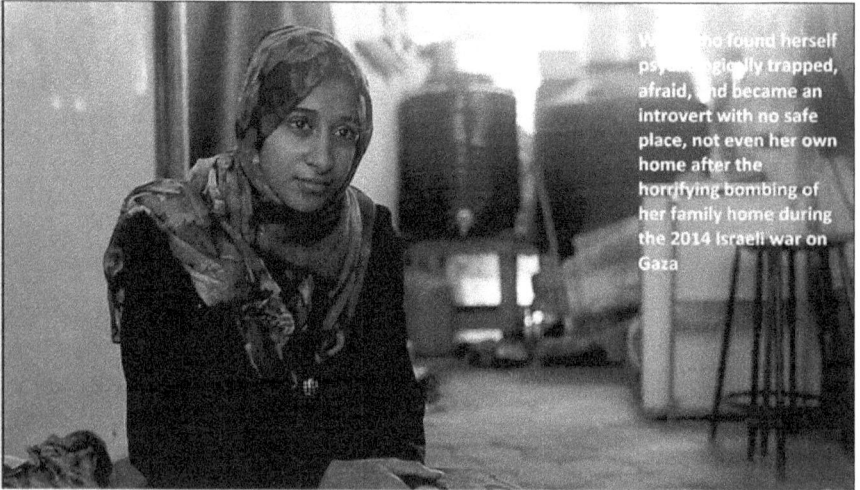

W... who found herself
ps... ...gically trapped,
afraid, ...nd became an
introvert with no safe
place, not even her own
home after the
horrifying bombing of
her family home during
the 2014 Israeli war on
Gaza

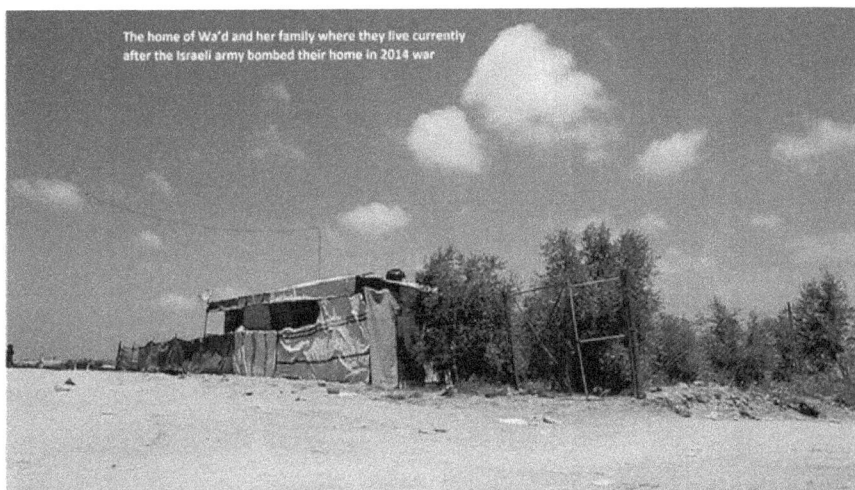

The home of Wa'd and her family where they live currently after the Israeli army bombed their home in 2014 war

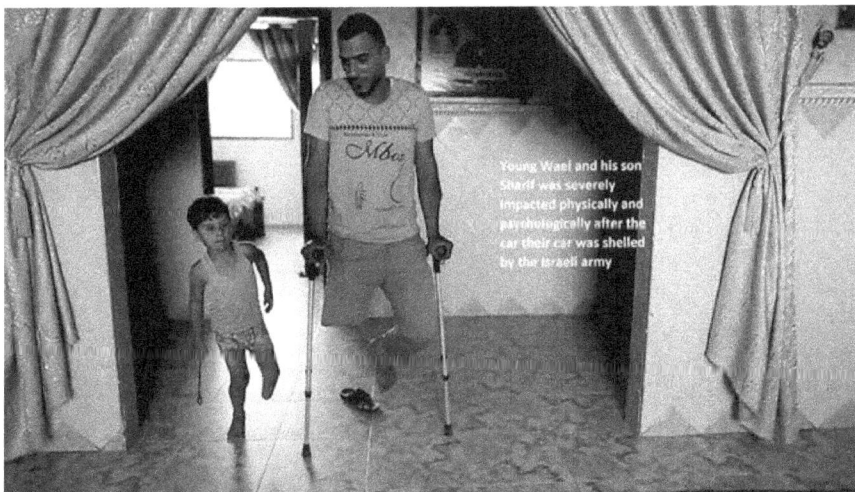

Young Wael and his son Sharif was severely impacted physically and psychologically after the car their car was shelled by the Israeli army

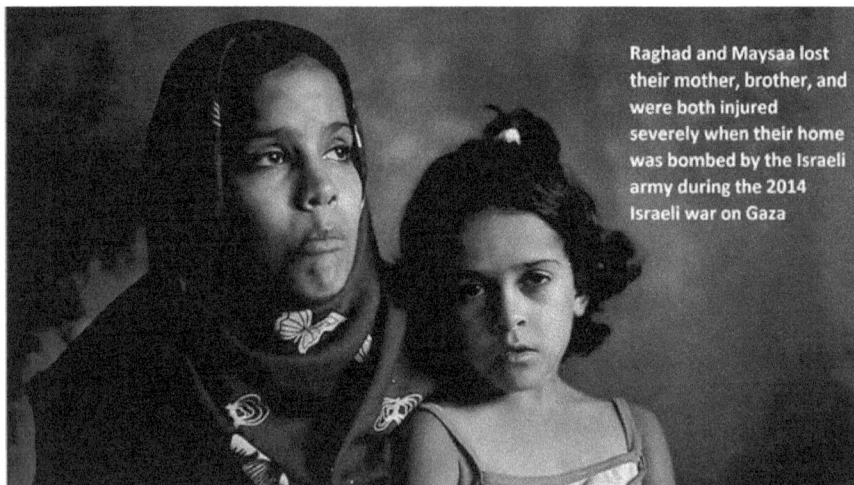

Raghad and Maysaa lost their mother, brother, and were both injured severely when their home was bombed by the Israeli army during the 2014 Israeli war on Gaza

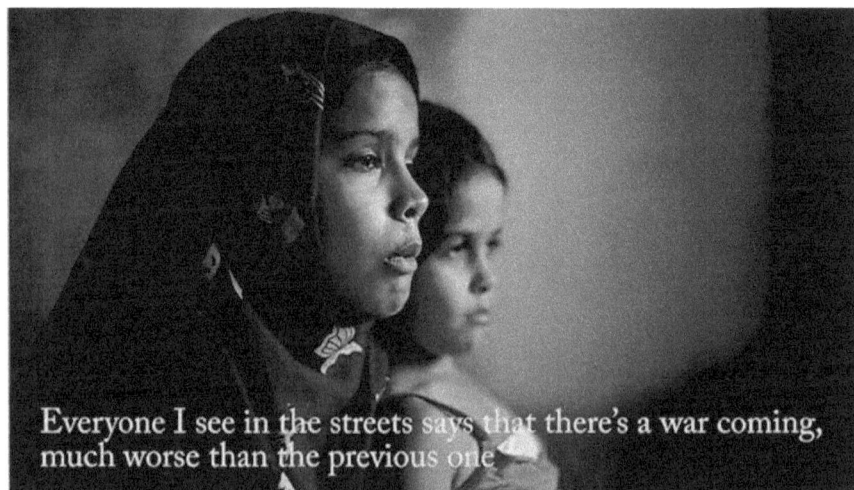

Everyone I see in the streets says that there's a war coming, much worse than the previous one

Palestinian kids message to the Israelis and the word "They want to live in peace and safety"

Palestinian kids message to the Israelis and the word "They want to live in peace and safety"

APPENDIX B:

Palestinian Children's Drawings

Mohammed

Raghad

Yazan

Yazan

Yazan

مخيم عودة

يزن

طائرة زنانة

قناص

دبابة

يوم رجل

جيب

شارع بكر

خيمة

أطفال

سيارة إسعاف

شباب

حمالة

Raghad

APPENDIX C:

Definition of Terms

The Gaza Strip: a small, self-governing Palestinian territory; its borders comprise of the Mediterranean Sea to the west, Egypt to the southwest, and Israel to the north and east.[255] The Gaza Strip, together with the West Bank, constitute the Palestinian territories occupied by Israeli occupation in the year 1967. The territories of the Gaza Strip and the West Bank are separated by territory occupied by Israeli occupation starting in 1948 when the Declaration of the Establishment of the State of Israel took place. In 1948, the main phase of the Arab-Israeli War began when the Arab League marched their forces into former British Palestine to support Palestinian Arabs.

Both the Gaza Strip and the West Bank fall under the jurisdiction of the Palestinian National Authority (PA). The PA was established in 1994 as the governing body of parts of the West bank and Gaza Strip. This occurred after the signing of the Oslo Accords between the Palestinian Liberation Organization (PLO) and Israel. Since June 2007, Hamas has been governing the Gaza Strip. At that point in 2007 the Israeli and U.S.-led international sanctions on the Gaza Strip were started. After decades of war, cease-fires, and peace accords, it has become the world's most intractable conflict, with the ongoing Israeli occupation of the West Bank and the Gaza Strip reaching 50 years.[256]

Lived experience: This term is "used in phenomenological studies to emphasize the importance of individual experiences of people as

---

[255] Roy, 2011.

[256] Cf. United Nations, 1997.

conscious human beings."[257] Lived experiences, as opposed to secondhand experiences, are experienced directly.[258]

PTSD: Post-traumatic stress disorder, which was officially classified around 1980 and applied to many U.S. Vietnam War veterans.

Trauma: Originally from the word "wound" in Greek and was applied for physical injury before it became used for psychological injury by the end of the 19th century.[259] The *Diagnostic and Statistical Manual of Mental Disorders* (DSM-5) defines trauma as "exposure to actual or threatened death, serious injury, or sexual violence."[260] Trauma is connected to the actual victim of threats, injury or violence, or to witnesses of those threats, injuries or violence.[261]

Traumatic event: According to the *DSM-5* a *traumatic event* requires all of the following diagnostic criteria: "exposure to actual or threatened death, serious injury, or sexual violence in one (or more) of the following ways: 1. Directly experiencing the event(s); 2. Witnessing, in person, the event(s) as it occurred to others; 3. Learning that the traumatic event(s) occurred to a close family member or close friend …; 4. Experiencing repeated or extreme exposure to aversive details of the traumatic event(s)."[262]

---

[257] Creswell, 1007.

[258] Patton, 2002.

[259] Breuer & S. Freud, 1895/1955.

[260] *DSM-5,* American Psychiatric Association, 2013, p. 271.

[261] APA, 2013

[262] *DSM-5,* American Psychiatric Association, 2013.

APPENDIX D:

Historical Timeline of Palestine

63 BCE Romans occupy Palestine

66 CE–136 CE The Jewish-Roman wars take place

634 Muslim troops take control of Palestine

687–691 The Dome of the Rock is built in Jerusalem

c. 800 The Jewish High Council moves to Jerusalem

1075 The Seljuk armies take Palestine

1096–1099 The First Crusade takes place

1100 The Kingdom of Jerusalem is formed

1187 Salah al-Din captures Jerusalem from the Crusaders

1244 The Khwarezmians capture Jerusalem

1291–1517 The Mamluks control the region

1517 The Ottomans take Palestine

1799 The Napoleonic Wars take place

1808–1810 The arrival of the current Jewish Ashkenazi community in the region

1837 The Palestinian peasants revolt against Egyptian conscription and taxation policies in Palestine because of the elimination of the unofficial rights and privileges enjoyed by the various societal groups under Ottoman rule previously.

1901 The Jewish National Fund is established with the purpose of buying Ottoman-Syrian lands for a Jewish settlement there

1915 The Hussein-McMahon Correspondence

1916 Sykes-Picot Agreement

1916–1918 The Arab Revolt takes place

1917 Britain issues the Balfour Declaration

1929 The outbreak of the Palestine riots

1948 The State of Israel is formed

1964 The PLO is founded

1967 The Six-Day War takes place

1973 The Yom Kippur War takes place

1980 The Israeli government declares Jerusalem its capital

1982 The First Lebanon War takes place

1987–1991 The First Intifada takes place

1992 The Bush Administration holds up $10 billion in U.S. loan-guarantees to Israeli occupation in an attempt to limit Israeli settlement building on Palestinian lands

1993   The Oslo Peace Accords is signed

1994   The Palestinian Authority is established in Gaza and Jericho

2000–2005 The Second Intifada takes place

2002 The reoccupation of Palestinian areas begins

2004   The International Court of Justice rules that Israel's "separation barrier" routes violate international law

2006   The Second Lebanon War takes place

2007   Palestinian Unity Government is formed

2008   Israeli occupation initiates Operation Cast Lead in Gaza

2016   UN Security Council resolution 2334 condemns Israeli occupation of Palestinian lands

2012   Israeli forces launch a large-scale military attack on Gaza

2014   Israeli occupation launches Operation Protective Edge on the Gaza Strip

2017   The United States recognizes Jerusalem as the capital of Israeli occupation.

2021   Israeli military conducts airstrikes on four high-rise towers in Gaza City

2023   The oppression of Palestinians by the Israeli occupation regime continues. There are some 7 million Palestinian refugees and displaced persons worldwide

2024   After the October 7th attacks, Israeli occupation invades Gaza Strip killing over 28,064 civilians and the genocide against the Palestinians continues to take more innocent lives (As of February 10th, 2024 during the writing of this book)

References

Abou-Dagga, S. K. (2013). *Psychological stress and resilience among parents of autistic children in Gaza Strip* (Unpublished master's thesis). Islamic University, Gaza, Palestine.

Abu Tawahina, M. (2018). The Impact of Israeli Siege on Gaza Strip's Family Structures and Social Fabric. Mediterranean Journal of Social Sciences, 9(2), 197-204.

Abu-Saba, M. B. (1999). War-related trauma and stress characteristics of American University of Beirut students. *Journal of Traumatic Stress*, *12*(1), 201-207. doi:10.1023/A:1024766920789

AFP & TOI Staff. (2018, June 19). Israeli use of live fire in Gaza causing 'unprecedented crisis,' Red Cross says. *The Times of Israel*. Retrieved from https://www.timesofisrael.com/israeli-use-of-live-fire-in-gaza-causing-unprecedented-crisis-red-cross-says/

Ahmad, A. (1992). Symptoms of posttraumatic stress disorder among displaced Kurdish children in Iraq-victims of a man-made disaster after the Gulf war. *Nordic Journal of Psychiatry*, *46*(5), 315-319.

Ahmad, A., Sofi, M. A., Sundelin-Wahlsten, V., & Von Knorring, A. L. (2000). Posttraumatic stress disorder in children after the military operation "Anfal" in Iraqi Kurdistan. *European Child & Adolescent Psychiatry*, *9*(4), 235-243. doi:10.1007/s007870070026

Ajdukovic, M. (1998). Displaced adolescents in Croatia: Sources of stress and posttraumatic stress reaction. *Adolescence*, *33*(129), 209-218.

Akram, F. & Rudoren, J. (2014, August 24). Teenager Cites Ordeal as Captive of Israelis. *The New York Times*. Retrieved from https://www.nytimes.com/2014/08/25/world/middleeast/gaza-strip-palestinian-teenager-cites-ordeal-as-captive-of-israelis-soldiers.html

Al Jazeera. (2018, June 04). *Save the children: Gaza children on brink of mental health crisis*. Retrieved from https://www.aljazeera.com/

news/2018/06/save-children-gaza-children-brink-mental-health-crisis-180603190059320.html

Al Mezan Center For Human Rights. (2016, August 29). *Gaza two years on: 27 cases of suspected war crimes, 0 indictments.* Retrieved from http://www.mezan.org/en/post/21503/Gaza Two Years On:27 cases of suspected war crimes, 0 indictments

Albertyn, R., Bickler, S. W., Van As, A. B., Millar, A. J. W., & Rode, H. (2003). The effects of war on children in Africa. *Pediatric Surgery International, 19*(4), 227-232.

Alderson, P., & Morrow, V. (2011). *The ethics of research with children and young people: A practical handbook.* London, England: Sage. doi:10.4135/9781446268377

Al-Haddad, G. (2017, September 26). Gaza: Children suffer from war trauma three years on. *Al Jazeera.* https://www.aljazeera.com/features/2017/9/26/gaza-children-suffer-from-war-trauma-three-years-on

Allen, J. G. (2008). *Coping with trauma: Hope through understanding.* Washington, DC: American Psychiatric Publishing.

Altawil, M., Harrold, D., & Samara, M. (2008, January). Children of War in Palestine. *Children in War.* Retrieved from https://spcaltawil.com/public/storage/ArticlesFiles/AVA6lA9Nf7xGDLTAXNXrZ9Igyhm niAp2qv6O6K7k.pdf

Altawil, M., Nel, P. W., Asker, A., Samara, M., & Harrold, D. (2008). The effects of chronic war trauma among Palestinian children. *Children: The invisible victims of war. An interdisciplinary study.* Peterborough, England: DSM Technical Publications.

American Psychiatric Association (APA). (2013). *Diagnostic and statistical manual of mental disorders* (5th ed.). Washington, DC: American Psychiatric Association. doi:10.1176/appi.books.9780890425596

Amnesty International. (2023, June 20). Israel/OPT: Civilian deaths and extensive destruction in latest Gaza offensive highlight human toll of apartheid.

Amnesty International. (n.d.). Six Months On: Gaza's Great March of Return. Retrieved from https://www.amnesty.org/en/latest/campaigns/2018/10/gaza-great-march-of-return/

Andrews, T. (2012). What is social constructionism? *Grounded Theory Review*, *11*(1), 39-46.

Angel, B., Hjern, A., & Ingleby, D. (2001). Effects of war and organized violence on children: A study of Bosnian refugees in Sweden. *American Journal of Orthopsychiatry*, *71*(1), 4. doi:10.1037/0002-9432.71.1.4

Arroyo, W., & Eth, S. (1985). Children traumatized by Central American warfare. In S. Eth & R. S. Pynoos (Eds.), *Post-traumatic stress disorder in children* (pp.101-120). Washington, DC: American Psychiatric Press.

Assmann, J. (2011). Cultural Memory and Early Civilization: Writing, Remembrance, and Political Imagination. Cambridge University Press.

Attanayake, V., McKay, R., Joffres, M., Singh, S., Burkle, F., & Mills, E. (2009). Prevalence of mental disorders among children exposed to war: a systematic review of 7,920 children. Medicine, Conflict, and Survival, 25(1), 4-19.

B'Tselem. (2002, May). *Land grab: Israel's settlement policy in the West Bank. Jerusalem: B'Tselem—The Israeli Information Centre for Human Rights in the Occupied Territories.* Retrieved from http://www.btselem.org/English/Publications/Summaries/200205_Land_Grab.asp

B'Tselem. (n.d.). *Fatalities during Operation Cast Lead.* Retrieved from https://www.btselem.org/statistics/fatalities/during-cast-lead/by-date-of-event

Baker, A. M. (1990). The psychological impact of the Intifada on Palestinian children in the occupied West Bank and Gaza: An exploratory study. *American Journal of Orthopsychiatry*, *60*(4), 496.

Baker, A., & Shalhoub-Kevorkian, N. (1999). Effects of political and military traumas on children: The Palestinian case. *Clinical Psychology Review*, *19*(8), 935-950. doi:10.1016/S0272-7358(99)00004-5

Bandura, A. (1978). Social learning theory of aggression. *Journal of Communication*, *28*(3), 12–29.

Barber, B. K. (2008). *Adolescents and war: How youth deal with political violence.* New York, NY: Oxford University Press.

Barker, C., & Pistrang, N. (2015). *Research methods in clinical psychology: An introduction for students and practitioners.* Chichester, England: John Wiley.

Barnett, M. N., & Finnemore, M. (1999). The politics, power, and pathologies of international organizations. *International Organization, 53*(4), 699-732. doi:10.1162/002081899551048

Barsella, A. (2006). *Barred from contact: Violations of the right to visit Palestinians held in Israeli prisons.* Jerusalem, Israel: B'Tselem.

Baumeister, R. F., & Vohs, K. D. (2002). The pursuit of meaningfulness in life. In C. R. Snyder & S. J. Lopez (Eds.), *Handbook of positive psychology* (pp. 608-618). New York, NY: University Press.

Berman, H. (2001). Children and war: Current understandings and future directions. *Public Health Nursing, 18*(4), 243-252. doi:10.1046/j.1525-1446.2001.00243.x

Betancourt, T. S., Borisova, I. I., Williams, T. P., Meyers-Ohki, S. E., Rubin-Smith, J. E., Annan, J., ... & Kohrt, B. A. (2010). Sierra Leone's former child soldiers: A follow-up study of psychosocial adjustment and community reintegration. Child Development, 81(4), 1077-1095.

Betancourt, T. S., Borisova, I. I., Williams, T. P., Meyers-Ohki, S. E., Rubin-Smith, J. E., Annan, J., ... & Kohrt, B. A. (2010). Sierra Leone's former child soldiers: A follow-up study of psychosocial adjustment and community reintegration. Child Development, 81(4), 1077-1095.

Blair, R. J. R. (1997). Moral reasoning and the child with psychopathic tendencies. *Personality and Individual Differences, 22*(5), 731-739. doi:10.1016/S0191-8869(96)00249-8

Bogdan, R., & Biklen, S. K. (1997). *Qualitative research for education.* Boston, MA: Allyn & Bacon.

Boothby, N. (1992). Displaced children: Psychological theory and practice from the field. *Journal of Refugee Studies, 5*(2), 106-122. doi:10.1093/jrs/5.2.106

Boxer, P., Rowell Huesmann, L., Dubow, E. F., Landau, S. F., Gvirsman, S. D., Shikaki, K., & Ginges, J. (2013). Exposure to violence across the social ecosystem and the development of aggression: A test of ecological theory in the Israeli–Palestinian conflict. *Child Development, 84*(1), 163-177. doi:10.1111/j.1467-8624.2012.01848.x

Boyden, J. (2003). Children under fire: Challenging assumptions about children's resilience. *Children Youth and Environments, 13*(1), 1-29.

Breuer, J., & Freud, S. (1955). Studies on hysteria. In J. Strachey (Ed. & Trans.), *The standard edition of the complete psychological works of Sigmund Freud* (Vol. 2, pp. 1-335). London, England: Hogarth Press. (Original work published 1895)

Brewin, C. R., Dalgleish, T., & Joseph, S. (1996). A dual representation theory of posttraumatic stress disorder. *Psychological Review, 103*(4), 670.

Briere, J., & Jordan, C. E. (2009). Childhood maltreatment, intervening variables, and adult psychological difficulties in women: An overview. *Trauma, Violence, & Abuse, 10*(4), 375-388. doi:10.1177/1524838009339757

Briere, J., Hodges, M., & Godbout, N. (2010). Traumatic stress, affect dysregulation, and dysfunctional avoidance: A structural equation model. *Journal of Traumatic Stress, 23*(6), 767-774.

Bronfenbrenner, U. (2005). Making human beings human: Bioecological perspectives on human development. Sage Publications.

Cairns, E., & Dawes, A. (1996). Children: Ethnic and political violence–a commentary. *Child Development, 67*(1), 129-139.

Camic, P. M., Rhodes, J. E., & Yardley, L. E. (2003). *Qualitative research in psychology: Expanding perspectives in methodology and design* Washington, DC: American Psychological Association. doi:10.1037/10595-000

Cannon, W. B. (1927). The James-Lange Theory of Emotions: A Critical Examination and an Alternative Theory. *The American Journal of Psychology, 39*(1/4), 106-124.

Carroll-Lind, J., Chapman, J., & Raskauskas, J. (2011). Children's perceptions of violence: The nature, extent and impact of their experiences. *Social Policy Journal of New Zealand, 37*, 6-19.

Catastrophic. (n.d.). In *Oxford living dictionaries*. Retrieved from https://en.oxforddictionaries.com/definition/catastrophic

Charara, R., Forouzanfar, M., Naghavi, M., Moradi-Lakeh, M., Afshin, A., Vos, T., . . . Hamadeh, R. R. (2017). The burden of mental disorders in the eastern Mediterranean region, 1990-2013. *PloS One*, *12*(1), e0169575. doi:10.1371/journal.pone.0169575

Children in the State of Palestine. (n.d.). Www.unicef.org. https://www.unicef.org/sop/reports/children-state-palestine-0

Churchill, S. D., & Wertz, F. J. (2001). An introduction to phenomenological research in psychology: Historical, conceptual, and methodological foundations. In K. J. Schneider, J. F. T. Bugental, & J. F. Pierson (Eds.), *Handbook* of *humanistic psychology*: *Leading edges* in *theory*, *research*, and *practice* (pp. 247-262). London, England: Sage.

Clausewitz, Carl von. "On War." Edited and translated by Michael Howard and Peter Paret. Princeton University Press, 1989.

Cloitre, M., Cohen, L. R., & Scarvalone, P. (2002). Understanding revictimization among childhood sexual abuse survivors: An interpersonal schema approach. *Journal of Cognitive Psychotherapy*, *16*(1), 91. doi:10.1891/jcop.16.1.91.63698

Conroy, S. A. (2003). A pathway for interpretive phenomenology. *International Journal of Qualitative Methods*, *2*(3), 36-62.

Cox, M. J., & Paley, B. (1997). Families as systems. *Annual Review of Psychology*, *48*(1), 243-267.

Creswell, J. W. (1998, 2007). *Qualitative inquiry and research design: Choosing among five approaches*. Los Angeles, CA: Sage.

Creswell, J. W. (2013). *Research design: Qualitative, quantitative, and mixed methods approaches*. Los Angeles, CA: Sage.

Creswell, J. W., & Plano, V. L. (2011). *Designing and conducting mixed methods research*. Los Angeles, CA: Sage.

Creswell, J. W., Hanson, W. E., Clark Plano, V. L., & Morales, A. (2007). Qualitative research designs: Selection and implementation. *The Counseling Psychologist*, *35*(2), 236-264.

Cruickshank, W. M., Bentzen, F. A., Ratzeburg, F. H., & Tannhauser, M. T. (1961). *A teaching method for brain injured and hyperactive children:*

A demonstration pilot study. Syracuse, NY: Syracuse University Press.

Dalgleish, T., Taghavi, R., Neshat-Doost, H., Moradi, A., Canterbury, R., & Yule, W. (2003). Patterns of processing bias for emotional information across clinical disorders: A comparison of attention, memory, and prospective cognition in children and adolescents with depression, generalized anxiety, and posttraumatic stress disorder. *Journal of Clinical Child and Adolescent Psychology, 32*(1), 10-21. doi:10.1207/15374420360533022

Danieli, Y. (1998). International Handbook of Multigenerational Legacies of Trauma. Plenum Press.

Davis, C. G., & Nolen-Hoeksema, S. (2001). Loss and meaning: How do people make sense of loss? *American Behavioral Scientist, 44*(5), 726-741.

Dawes, A. (1990). The effects of political violence on children—a consideration of South African and related studies. *International Journal of Psychology, 25*(1), 13-31.

De Jong, K., Mulhern, M., Ford, N., Van Der Kam, S., & Kleber, R. (2000). The trauma of war in Sierra Leone. *Lancet, 355*(9220), 2067-2068.

Defense for Children International Palestine (DCIP). (2014, July 24). *July 24 update: Death toll of Palestinian children spirals as Israel expands Gaza offensive.* Retrieved from https://www.dci-palestine. org/july_24_update_death_toll_of_palestinian_children_ spirals_as_israel_expands_gaza_offensive

Deković, M., & Meeus, W. (1997). Peer relations in adolescence: Effects of parenting and adolescents' self-concept. Journal of Adolescence, 20(2), 163-176.

Dimitry, I. (2012), A systematic review on the mental health of children and adolescents in areas of armed conflict in the Middle East. *Child. Care, Health and Development, 38*(2), 153-161.

Dunmore, E., Clark, D. M., & Ehlers, A. (2001). A prospective investigation of the role of cognitive factors in persistent posttraumatic stress disorder (PTSD) after physical or sexual assault. *Behaviour Research and Therapy, 39*(9), 1063-1084.

Dyregrov, A., Gjestad, R., & Raundalen, M. (2002). Children exposed to warfare: A longitudinal study. *Journal of Traumatic Stress*, *15*(1), 59-68.

Ehntholt, K. A., Smith, P. A., & Yule, W. (2005). School-based cognitive-behavioural therapy group intervention for refugee children who have experienced war-related trauma. *Clinical Child Psychology and Psychiatry*, *10*(2), 235-250.

Eisenbruch, M. (1991). From post-traumatic stress disorder to cultural bereavement: Diagnosis of Southeast Asian refugees. *Social Science & Medicine*, *33*(6), 673-680.

Elbedour, S., Onwuegbuzie, A. J., Ghannam, J., Whitcome, J. A., & Hein, F. A. (2007). Post-traumatic stress disorder, depression, and anxiety among Gaza Strip adolescents in the wake of the second Uprising (Intifada). Child Abuse & Neglect, 31(7), 719-729.

El-Khosondar, I. (2004). *The effect of rational behaviour therapy in reducing the effect of post-traumatic stress disorder among Palestinian children* (Unpublished doctoral dissertation). Ain Shams University, Cairo, Egypt.

El-Sarraj, E., & Qouta, S. (2005). The Palestinian experience. Disasters and mental health. In J. J. López-Ibor, G. Christodoulou, M. Maj, N. Sartorius, & A. Okasha (Eds.), *Disasters and mental health* (Vol. 4, pp. 229-237). Chichester, England: John Wiley.

Emotion. (2018). *The American Heritage dictionary*. Retrieved from https://ahdictionary.com/word/search.html?q=emotion

Essential Statistics. (n.d.). Defense for Children Palestine. Retrieved October 4, 2023, from https://www.dci-palestine.org/essential_statistics

Eth, S. (Ed.). (2008). *PTSD in children and adolescents* (Vol. 20). Washington, DC: American Psychiatric Publishing.

Farhood, L., Zurayk, H., Chaya, M., Saadeh, F., Meshefedjian, G., & Sidani, T. (1993). The impact of war on the physical and mental health of the family: The Lebanese experience. *Social Science & Medicine*, *36*(12), 1555-1567.

Fathi, R., Bakr, R., & Gharaibeh, H. (2013). War stress and psychological trauma: Mental health of Palestinian children. The Arab Journal of Psychiatry, 24(2), 167-176.

Feldman, R., & Vengrober, A. (2011). Posttraumatic stress disorder in infants and young children exposed to war-related trauma. *Journal of the American Academy of Child & Adolescent Psychiatry, 50*(7), 645-658.

Fisher, L., & Blair, R. J. R. (1998). Cognitive impairment and its relationship to psychopathic tendencies in children with emotional and behavioral difficulties. *Journal of Abnormal Child Psychology, 26*(6), 511-519.

Foa, E. B., Steketee, G., & Rothbaum, B. O. (1989). Behavioral/cognitive conceptualizations of post-traumatic stress disorder. *Behavior Therapy, 20*(2), 155-176.

Folkman, S., Lazarus, R. S., Gruen, R. J., & DeLongis, A. (1986). Appraisal, coping, health status, and psychological symptoms. *Journal of Personality and Social Psychology, 50*(3), 571.

Freh, F. M. (2015). Psychological effects of war and violence on children. *Journal of Psychological Abnormalities, 4*, e106. doi:10.4172/2329-9525.1000e106

Freire, P. (1970). Pedagogy of the Oppressed. Herder and Herder.

Freud, A., & Burlingham, D. (1943). *Children and war*. New York, NY: Ernst Willard.

Freud, S. (1960). *Jokes and their relation to the unconscious* (J. Strachey, Trans.). New York, NY: Holt, Rinehart, Winston.

Fuchs, E. C., & Thelen, T. (2008). Remembering the Second World War in Europe. Contemporary European History, 17(2), 213-224.

Garbarino, J., & Kostelny, K. (1996). The effects of political violence on Palestinian children's behavior problems: A risk accumulation model. *Child Development, 67*(1), 33-45.

Garbarino, J., Kostelny, K., & Dubrow, N. (1991a). What children can tell us about living in danger. *American Psychologist, 46*(4), 376.

Garbarino, J., Kostelny, K., & Dubrow, N. (1991b). *No place to be a child: Growing up in a war zone*. Lexington, MA: Lexington Books.

Garrick, T., Morrow, N., Shalev, A. Y., & Eth, S. (2001). Stress-induced enhancement of auditory startle: An animal model of posttraumatic stress disorder. *Psychiatry: Interpersonal and Biological Processes, 64*(4), 346-354. doi:10.1521/psyc.64.4.346.18600

Gerring, J. P., Brady, K. D., Chen, A., Vasa, R., Grados, M., Bandeen-Roche, K., & Bryan, N. (1998). Premorbid prevalence of ADHD and development of secondary ADHD after closed head injury. *Journal of the American Academy of Child & Adolescent Psychiatry, 37*(6), 647-654. https://doi.org/10.1097/00004583-199806000-00016

Giorgi, A. (1997). The theory, practice, and evaluation of the phenomenological method as a qualitative research procedure. *Journal of Phenomenological Psychology, 28*(2), 235-260. doi:10.1163/156916297X00103

Giorgi, A. (1999). A phenomenological perspective on some phenomenographic results on learning. *Journal of Phenomenological Psychology, 30*(2), 68-93.

Giorgi, A. (Ed.). (1985). *Phenomenology and psychological research.* Pittsburgh, PA: Duquesne University Press.

Giorgi, A. P., & Giorgi, B. (2008). Phenomenological psychology. In C. Willig & W. Stainton-Rogers (Eds.), *The SAGE handbook of qualitative research in psychology* (pp. 165-179). London, England: Sage.

Goldstein, R. D., Wampler, N. S., & Wise, P. H. (1997). War experiences and distress symptoms of Bosnian children. *Pediatrics, 100*(5), 873-878.

Gorman-Smith, D., & Tolan, P. (1998). The role of exposure to community violence and developmental problems among inner-city youth. *Development and Psychopathology, 10*(1), 101-116. doi:10.1017/S0954579498001539

Hawajri, A. (2003). *Effectiveness of a suggested counseling program to alleviate trauma among the students of basic stage in Gaza Governorate* (Unpublished dissertation). Islamic University, Gaza, Palestine.

Hein, F. A., Qouta, S., Thabet, A., & El Sarraj, E. (1993). Trauma and mental health of children in Gaza. *British Medical Journal, 306*(6885), 1130. doi:10.1136/bmj.306.6885.1130-c

Holloway, I. (1997). *Basic concepts for qualitative research.* Oxford, England: Blackwell Science.

Hooven, C., Nurius, P. S., Logan-Greene, P., & Thompson, E. A. (2012). Childhood violence exposure: Cumulative and specific effects on adult mental health. *Journal of Family Violence, 27*(6), 511-522. https://info.wafa.ps/ar_page.aspx?id=y7SojLa913397354Iay7SojL

Hubbard, J., Realmuto, G. M., Northwood, A. K., & Masten, A. S. (1995). Comorbidity of psychiatric diagnoses with posttraumatic stress disorder in survivors of childhood trauma. *Journal of the American Academy of Child & Adolescent Psychiatry, 34*(9), 1167-1173. doi:10.1097/00004583-199509000-00014

Humaid, M. (n.d.). *A year on from war, Gaza frustrated at slow reconstruction.* Www.aljazeera.com. https://www.aljazeera.com/news/2022/5/10/year-on-war-gaza-frustrated-slow-reconstruction

Human Rights Watch (HRW). (2019). Israel/Palestine: Israeli Army Demolishing West Bank Schools. Retrieved from https://www.hrw.org/news/2019/04/24/israel/palestine-israeli-army-demolishing-west-bank-schools.

Human Rights Watch. (2009). "White Flag Deaths: Killings of Palestinian Civilians during Operation Cast Lead." https://www.hrw.org/report/2009/08/13/white-flag-deaths/killings-palestinian-civilians-during-operation-cast-lead

Human Rights Watch. (2017). *World report 2017 events of 2016* (Report No. 27, pp. 363-354). New York, NY: Author. doi:https://www.hrw.org/sites/default/files/world_report_download/wr2017-web.pdf

Husserl, E. (1970). *Logical investigations* (J. N. Findlay, Trans.). New York, NY: Humanities Press.

Institute for Middle East Understanding (IMEU). (2014, August 28). *The Children of Gaza: A Generation Scarred & Under Siege.* Retrieved from https://imeu.org/article/the-children-of-gaza-a-generation-scarred-under-siege

Institute for Middle East Understanding (IMEU). (2014, February 6). *Israeli violations of Palestinian academic freedom & access to education.* Retrieved from https://imeu.org/article/israeli-violations-of-palestinian-academic-freedom-access-to-education

Institute for Middle East Understanding (IMEU). (2014, September 10). *50 Days of Death & Destruction: Israel's "Operation Protective*

Edge." Retrieved from https://imeu.org/article/50-days-of-death-destruction-israels-operation-protective-edge

Israel/OPT: Civilian deaths and extensive destruction in latest Gaza offensive highlight human toll of apartheid. (2023, June 13). Amnesty International. https://www.amnesty.org/en/latest/news/2023/06/israel-opt-civilian-deaths-and-extensive-destruction-in-latest-gaza-offensive-highlight-human-toll-of-apartheid/ "Children in the State of Palestine." https://www.unicef.org/oPt/reports/children-state-palestine.

Javidi, H., & Yadollahie, M. (2012). Post-traumatic stress disorder. *International Journal of Occupational and Environmental Medicine, 3*(1), 2-9.

Jensen, P. S., & Shaw, J. (1993). Children as victims of war: Current knowledge and future research needs. *Journal of the American Academy of Child & Adolescent Psychiatry, 32*(4), 697-708. doi:10.1097/00004583-199307000-00001

Joseph, S., Williams, R., & Yule, W. (1997). *Understanding post-traumatic stress: A psychosocial perspective on PTSD and treatment.* Chichester, England: Wiley.

Just Vision. (n.d.). Hammas-Fatah conflict. Retrieved from https://justvision.org/glossary/hamas-fatah-conflict

Kaminer, D., Stein, M. B., & Kleinman, A. (2000). Posttraumatic stress disorder: The missed diagnosis. Journal of Nervous and Mental Disease, 188(12), 803-806.

Kaniasty, K., & Norris, F. H. (2008). Longitudinal linkages between perceived social support and posttraumatic stress symptoms: Sequential roles of social causation and social selection. Journal of Traumatic Stress, 21(3), 274-281.

Keresteš, G. (2006). Children's aggressive and prosocial behavior in relation to war exposure: Testing the role of perceived parenting and child's gender. *International Journal of Behavioral Development, 30*(3), 227-239. doi:10.1177/0165025406066756

Khamis, V. (2011). The emotional experience of Palestinians during the 2008–2009 war in Gaza. Peace and Conflict: Journal of Peace Psychology, 17(3), 246-266.

Khamis, V. (2015). Coping with war trauma and psychological distress among school-age Palestinian children. *American Journal of Orthopsychiatry, 85*(1), 72. doi:10.1037/ort0000039

Khamis, V. (2018). Psychological distress and coping among Palestinian children: A mixed-methods approach. Vulnerable Children and Youth Studies, 13(1), 58-70.

Kinzie, J. D. (2001). The Southeast Asian refugee: The legacy of severe trauma. In W. S. Tseng & J. Streltzer (Eds.), *Culture and psychotherapy: A guide to clinical practice* (Vol. 191, pp.173-191). Washington DC: American Psychiatric Publishing.

Kinzie, J. D., Sack, W. H., Angell, R. H., Manson, S., & Rath, B. (1986). The psychiatric effects of massive trauma on Cambodian children: I. The children. *Journal of the American Academy of Child Psychiatry, 25*(3), 370-376. doi:10.1016/S0002-7138(09)60259-4

Kira, I. A., Ashby, J. S., Lewandowski, L., Alawneh, A. W. N., Mohanesh, J., & Odenat, L. (2013). Advances in continuous traumatic stress theory: Traumatogenic dynamics and consequences of intergroup conflict: The Palestinian adolescents case. *Psychology, 4*(04), 396.

Konrad, K., Gauggel, S., Manz, A., & Schöll, M. (2000). Inhibitory control in children with traumatic brain injury (TBI) and children with attention deficit/hyperactivity disorder (ADHD). *Brain Injury, 14*(10), 859-875. doi:10.1080/026990500445691

Kostelny, K., & Garbarino, J. (2001). The war close to home: Children and violence in the United States. In D. J. Christie, R. V. Wagner, & D. D. N. Winter (Eds.), *Peace, conflict, and violence: Peace psychology for the 21st century* (pp. 110-119). Upper Saddle River, NJ: Prentice Hall/Pearson Education.

Kruger, D., & Stones, C. R. (1981). *An introduction to phenomenological psychology*. Pittsburgh, PA: Duquesne University Press.

Kvale, S. (1997). *Interviews. An introduction to qualitative research interviewing*. Thousand Oaks, CA: Sage.

Kvale, S., & Brinkmann, S. (2009). *Interviews: Learning the craft of qualitative research*. Thousand Oaks, CA: Sage.

Laor, N., Wolmer, L., & Cohen, D. J. (2001). Mothers' functioning and children's symptoms 5 years after a SCUD missile attack. *American Journal of Psychiatry*, *158*(7), 1020-1026. doi:10.1176/appi. ajp.158.7.1020

Lasser, J., & Adams, K. (2007). The effects of war on children: School psychologists' role and function. *School Psychology International*, *28*(1), 5-10.

Leavitt, L. A., & Fox, N. A. (2014). *The psychological effects of war and violence on children*. New York, NY: Psychology Press.

LeDoux, J. (1996). The Emotional Brain: The Mysterious Underpinnings of Emotional Life. Simon & Schuster.

Lodico, M. G., Spaulding, D. T., & Voegtle, K. H. (2010). *Methods in educational research: From theory to practice* (Vol. 28). San Francisco, CA: Jossey-Bass, Wiley Imprint.

Machel, G. (2001). *The impact of war on children: A review of progress since the 1996 United Nations report on the impact of armed conflict on children*. New York, NY: United Nations Children's Fund.

Maier, S. F., & Seligman, M. E. (1976). Learned helplessness: Theory and evidence. *Journal of Experimental Psychology: General*, *105*(1), 3. doi:10.1037/0096-3445.105.1.3

Margolin, G., & Gordis, E. B. (2000). The effects of family and community violence on children. Annual Review of Psychology, 51, 445-479.

Marlowe, Jen. (2015, July 2). Gaza's Mental-Health Crisis and the Trauma of Permanent War. *The Nation*. Retrieved from https://www.thenation. com/article/archive/gazas-mental-health-crisis-and-the-trauma-of-permanent-war/

Masten, A. S., & Coatsworth, J. D. (1998). The development of competence in favorable and unfavorable environments: Lessons from research on successful children. *American Psychologist*, *53*(2), 205. doi:10.1037/0003-066X.53.2.205

Max, J. E., Arndt, S., Castillo, C. S., Bokura, H., Robin, D. A., Lindgren, S. D., . . . Mattheis, P. J. (1998). Attention-deficit hyperactivity symptomatology after traumatic brain injury: A prospective study. *Journal of the American Academy of Child & Adolescent Psychiatry*, *37*(8), 841-847.

Maypole, J., & Davies, T. G. (2001). Students' perceptions of constructivist learning in a community college American History II survey course. *Community College Review, 29*(2), 54-79.

McGee, C. (2000). *Childhood experiences of domestic violence.* London, England: Jessica Kingsley.

McGrath, J. E., & Johnson, B. A. (2003). Methodology makes meaning: How both qualitative and quantitative paradigms shape evidence and its interpretation. In P. M. Camic, J. E. Rhodes, & L. Yardley (Eds.), *Qualitative research in psychology: Expanding perspectives in methodology and design* (pp. 31-48). Washington, DC: American Psychological Association. doi:10.1037/10595-003

Merriam, S. (1995). What can you tell from an N of l?: Issues of validity and reliability in qualitative research. *PAACE Journal of Lifelong Learning, 4,* 50-60.

Merriam, S. B., Tisdell, E., Taylor, K., Lamoreaux, A., & Clarke, M. (2009). Beyond andragogy: New directions in adult learning theory. *New Directions for Adult and Continuing Education, 119,* 455-461.

Mghir, R. I. M., Freed, W., Raskin, A., & Katon, W. (1995). Depression and posttraumatic stress disorder among a community sample of adolescent and young adult Afghan refugees. *Journal of Nervous and Mental Disease, 183*(1), 24-30. doi:10.1177/00207640990450010

Middle East Monitor. (2014, August 04). *Military Expert: Israel is using 3 internationally banned weapons in Gaza.* Retrieved from https://www.middleeastmonitor.com/ 20140804-military-expert-israel-is-using-3-internationally-banned-weapons-in-gaza/

Mihalic, S. W., & Elliott, D. (1997). A social learning theory model of marital violence. *Journal of Family Violence, 12*(1), 21-47.

Mollica, R. F., Poole, C., Son, L., Murray, C. C., & Tor, S. (1997). Effects of war trauma on Cambodian refugee adolescents' functional health and mental health status. *Journal of the American Academy of Child & Adolescent Psychiatry, 36*(8), 1098-1106. doi:10.1097/00004583-199708000-00017

More than 10,000 Palestinians killed in Israeli attacks on Gaza. (n.d.). Al
    Jazeera. https://www.aljazeera.com/news/2023/11/6/number-of-
    palestinians-killed-in-israeli-attacks-on-gaza-tops-10000

Mousa, F., & Madi, H. (2003). *Impact of the humanitarian crisis in the
    occupied Palestinian territory on people and services.* Gaza, Palestine:
    United Nations Relief and Works Agency for Palestinian Refugees
    in the Near East (UNRWA).

Moustakas, C. (1994). *Phenomenological research methods.* Thousand Oaks,
    CA: Sage.

Mudaly, N., & Goddard, C. (2009). The ethics of involving children who
    have been abused in child abuse research. *International Journal of
    Children's Rights, 17*(2), 261-281. doi:10.1163/157181808X389920}

Murthy, R. S., & Lakshminarayana, R. (2006). Mental health consequences
    of war: A brief review of research findings. *World Psychiatry, 5*(1), 25.

Murthy, R. S., & Srinivasa, R. (2007). Mass violence and mental health --
    Recent epidemiological findings. *International Review of Psychiatry,*
    19:3, 183 - 192. doi: 10.1080/09540260701365460

Nader, K. O., Pynoos, R. S., Fairbanks, L. A., Al-Ajeel, M., & Al-Asfour, A.
    (1993). A preliminary study of PTSD and grief among the children
    of Kuwait following the Gulf crisis. *British Journal of Clinical
    Psychology, 32*(4), 407-416. http://dx.doi:10.1111/j.2044-8260.1993.
    tb01075.x

Nader, K., Pynoos, R., Fairbanks, L., & Frederick, C. (1990). Children's
    PTSD reactions one year after a sniper attack at their school. *American
    Journal of Psychiatry, 147*(11), 1526. doi:10.1176/ajp.147.11.1526

Najjar, Farah. (2017, February 1). Gaza power crisis: 'We want to end this
    nightmare.' *Al Jazeera.* Retrieved from https://www.aljazeera.com/
    features/2017/2/1/gaza-power-crisis-we-want-to-end-this-nightmare

National Institute of Mental Health. (2015). *Helping children and adolescents
    cope with violence and disasters: What parents can do.* Retrieved from
    https://www.nimh.nih.gov/health/publications/helping-children-
    and-adolescents-cope-with-violence-and-disasters-parents/index.
    shtml

Neimeyer, R. A. (2003). Meaning reconstruction & the experience of loss.
    American Psychological Association.

Okasha, T., & Elkholy, H. (2012). A synopsis of recent influential papers published in psychiatric journals (2010–2011) from the Arab World. *Asian Journal of Psychiatry, 5*(2), 175-178. doi:10.1016/j.ajp.2012.05.001

Osofsky, J. D. (Ed.). (1998). *Children in a violent society.* New York, NY: Guilford Press.

Osofsky, J. D., Wewers, S., Hann, D. M., & Fick, A. C. (1993). Chronic community violence: What is happening to our children? *Psychiatry, 56*(1), 36-45. doi:10.1080/00332747.1993.11024619

Palestinian Center for Human Rights. (2020). "Psychosocial Support for Palestinian Children in the Gaza Strip: An Urgent Necessity." http://pchrgaza.org/en/?p=13753

Palestinian Centre for Human Rights (PCHR). (2014). *Annual report 2014* (pp. 1-248). Gaza, Palestine: United Nations Development Programme (UNDP). doi:http://www.undp.ps/en/newsroom/publications/pdf/other/gazaoneyear.pdf

Panter-Brick, C. (2015). Culture and resilience: Next steps for theory and practice. *Youth resilience and culture: Commonalities and complexities,* 233-244.

Patterson, C. M., & Newman, J. P. (1993). Reflectivity and learning from aversive events: Toward a psychological mechanism for the syndromes of disinhibition. *Psychological Review, 100*(4), 716. doi:10.1037/0033-295X.100.4.716

Patton, M. Q. (1990). *Qualitative evaluation and research methods.* Thousand Oaks, CA: Sage.

Patton, M. Q. (2002). *Qualitative research and evaluation methods* (3rd ed.). Thousand Oaks, CA: Sage.

Pearlman, L. A., & Courtois, C. A. (2005). Clinical applications of the attachment framework: Relational treatment of complex trauma. *Journal of Traumatic Stress: Official Publication of the International Society for Traumatic Stress Studies, 18*(5), 449-459.

Peled, E. (2010). Doing good in social work research: With or for participants? A commentary on: 'The obligation to bring about good in social work research: A new perspective.' *Qualitative Social Work, 9*(1), 21-26. doi:10.1177/1473325009355617

Powell, M. A., & Smith, A. B. (2009). Children's participation rights in research. *Childhood, 16*(1), 124-142.

Punamäki, R. L. (2009). War, military violence, and aggressive development: Child, family, and social preconditions. Adolescents and war: How youth deal with political violence. In B. K. Barber (Ed.), *Adolescents and war: How youth deal with political violence* (pp. 62-79). New York, NY: Oxford University Press.

Punamäki, R. L., & Suleiman, R. (1990). Predictors and effectiveness of coping with political violence among Palestinian children. *British Journal of Social Psychology, 29*(1), 67-77.

Punamäki, R. L., Qouta, S., & El Sarraj, E. (1997). Models of traumatic experiences and children's psychological adjustment: The roles of perceived parenting and the children's own resources and activity. *Child Development, 68*(4), 718-728. doi:10.1111/j.1467-8624.1997.tb04232.x

Punamäki, R. L., Qouta, S., & El-Sarraj, E. (2001). Resiliency factors predicting psychological adjustment after political violence among Palestinian children. *International Journal of Behavioral Development, 25*(3), 256-267. doi:10.1080/01650250042000294

Punamäki, R. L., Qouta, S., Sarraj, E. E., & Montgomery, E. (2006). Psychological distress and resources among siblings and parents exposed to traumatic events. *International Journal of Behavioral Development, 30*(5), 385-397.

Qouta, S. (2000). *Trauma, violence, and mental health: The Palestinian experience* (Unpublished doctoral dissertation). Vrije Universiteit, Amsterdam, Netherlands.

Qouta, S., & El Sarraj, E. (1992). Curfew and children's mental health. *Journal of Psychological Studies, 4*, 13-18.

Qouta, S., & El Sarraj, E. (2002). Community mental health as practiced by the Gaza Community Mental Health Programme. In J. de Jong (Ed.), *Trauma, war, and violence: Public mental health in socio-cultural context* (pp. 317-335). Boston, MA: Springer.

Qouta, S., & El Sarraj, E. (2004). Prevalence of PTSD among Palestinian children in Gaza Strip. *Arabpsynet Journal, 2*, 8-13.

Qouta, S., Punamäki, R. L., & El Sarraj, E. (1995a). The impact of the peace treaty on psychological well-being: A follow-up study of

Palestinian children. *Child Abuse & Neglect*, *19*(10), 1197-1208.

Qouta, S., Punamäki, R. L., & El Sarraj, E. (1995b). The relations between traumatic experiences, activity, and cognitive and emotional responses among Palestinian children. *International Journal of Psychology*, *30*(3), 289-304.

Qouta, S., Punamäki, R. L., & El Sarraj, E. (2003). Prevalence and determinants of PTSD among Palestinian children exposed to military violence. *European Child & Adolescent Psychiatry*, *12*(6), 265-272. doi:10.1007/s00787-003-0328-0

Qouta, S., Punamäki, R. L., & El Sarraj, E. (2005). Mother-child expression of psychological distress in war trauma. *Clinical Child Psychology and Psychiatry*, *10*(2), 135-156.

Qouta, S., Punamäki, R. L., & El Sarraj, E. (2008). Child development and family mental health in war and military violence: The Palestinian experience. *International Journal of Behavioral Development*, *32*(4), 310-321. doi:10.1177/0165025408090973

Qouta, S., Punamäki, R. L., & El Sarraj, E. (2008). Prevalence and determinants of PTSD among Palestinian children exposed to military violence. European Child & Adolescent Psychiatry, 17(4), 191-199.

Qouta, S., Punamäki, R. L., Miller, T., & El Sarraj, E. (2008). Does war beget child aggression? Military violence, gender, age and aggressive behavior in two Palestinian samples. *Aggressive Behavior: Official Journal of the International Society for Research on Aggression*, *34*(3), 231-244.

Ran, Y., Hadad, E., Daher, S., Ganor, O., Kohn, J., Yegorov, Y., . . . Hirschhorn, G. (2010). QuikClot combat gauze use for hemorrhage control in military trauma: January 2009 Israel Defense Force experience in the Gaza Strip: A preliminary report of 14 cases. *Prehospital and Disaster Medicine*, *25*(6), 584-588.

Realmuto, G. M., Masten, A., Carole, L. F., Hubbard, J., Groteluschen, A., & Chhun, B. (1992). Adolescent survivors of massive childhood trauma in Cambodia: Life events and current symptoms. *Journal of Traumatic Stress*, *5*(4), 589-599. doi:10.1007/BF00979227

Rees, C. A., Keane, T. M., & Shea, M. T. (2011). The relationship between war exposure, posttraumatic stress disorder symptoms, and the risk of intergenerational transmission of war trauma. Journal of Traumatic Stress, 24(4), 408-415.

Rought-Brooks, H. (2015). *Gaza: The impact of conflict on women.* Retrieved from https://www.nrc.no/globalassets/pdf/reports/gaza---the-impact-of-conflict-on-women.pdf

Roy, S. (2012). Reconceptualizing the Israeli-Palestinian conflict: Key paradigm shifts. *Journal of Palestine Studies, 41*(3), 71-91. doi:10.1525/jps.2012.XLI.3.71

Rubin, K. H., Coplan, R. J., & Bowker, J. C. (2009). Social withdrawal in childhood. *Annual Review of Psychology, 60*(2009), 141-171. doi:10.1146/annurev.psych.60.110707.163642

Rudestam, K. E., & Newton, R. R. (2014). *Surviving your dissertation: A comprehensive guide to content and process.* London, England: Sage.

Rutter, M., Tizard, J., Yule, W., Graham, P., & Whitmore, K. (1976). Isle of Wight studies, 1964–1974. *Psychological Medicine, 6*(2), 313-332.

Sack, W. H., Clarke, G. N., & Seeley, J. (1995). Posttraumatic stress disorder across two generations of Cambodian refugees. *Journal of the American Academy of Child & Adolescent Psychiatry, 34*(9), 1160-1166. doi:10.1097/00004583-199509000-00013

Sagi-Schwartz, A. (2008). The well-being of children living in chronic war zones: The Palestinian-Israeli case. *International Journal of Behavioral Development, 32*(4), 322-336. doi:10.1177/0165025408090974

Said, E. W. (1984). The World, the Text, and the Critic. Harvard University Press.

Saltzman, W. R., Layne, C. M., Steinberg, A. M., Arslanagic, B., & Pynoos, R. S. (2003). Developing a culturally and ecologically sound intervention program for youth exposed to war and terrorism. *Child and Adolescent Psychiatric Clinics of North America, 12*(2), 319-342. doi:10.1016/S1056-4993(02)00099-8

Save the Children. (2019). Life on the Frontline: The Impact of Conflict and the Humanitarian Response in Gaza on Children. Retrieved from https://www.savethechildren.org.uk/content/dam/gb/reports/emergencies/life-on-the-frontline.pdf

Schachter, S., & Singer, J. E. (1962). Cognitive, Social, and Physiological Determinants of Emotional State. Psychological Review, 69(5), 379-399.

Shaw, J. A. (2003). Children exposed to war/terrorism. *Clinical Child and Family Psychology Review, 6*(4), 237-246.

Shweder, R. A., & Bourne, E. J. (1982). Does the concept of the person vary cross-culturally? In R. A. Shweder & R. A. LeVine (Eds.), *Cultural conceptions of mental health and therapy* (pp. 97-137). Dordrecht, Netherlands: Springer.

Smith, P. K., Cowie, H., Olafsson, R. F., & Liefooghe, A. P. D. (2002). Definitions of bullying: A comparison of terms used, and age and gender differences, in a fourteen–country international comparison. Child Development, 73(4), 1119-1133.

Smith, P., Perrin, S., Yule, W., & Rabe-Hesketh, S. (2001). War exposure and maternal reactions in the psychological adjustment of children from Bosnia-Hercegovina. *Journal of Child Psychology and Psychiatry, 42*(3), 395-404. doi:10.1017/S0021963001007065

Smith, P., Perrin, S., Yule, W., Hacam, B., & Stuvland, R. (2002). War exposure among children from Bosnia-Hercegovina: Psychological adjustment in a community sample. *Journal of Traumatic Stress: Official Publication of the International Society for Traumatic Stress Studies, 15*(2), 147-156. doi:10.1023/A:1014812209051

Smith, P., Smith, C., Osborn, R., & Samara, M. (2008). A content analysis of school anti-bullying policies: Progress and limitations. *Educational Psychology in Practice, 24*(1), 1-12. doi:10.1080/02667360701661165

Springer, K. W., Sheridan, J., Kuo, D., & Carnes, M. (2007). Long-term physical and mental health consequences of childhood physical abuse: Results from a large population-based sample of men and women. *Child Abuse & Neglect, 31*(5), 517-530.

Stein, Yael. (2013, May). *Human Rights Violations during Operation Pillar of Defense: 14-21 November 2012.* B'Tselem. Retrieved from https://www.btselem.org/download/201305_pillar_of_defense_operation_eng.pdf

Stovall-McClough, K. C., & Cloitre, M. (2006). Unresolved attachment, PTSD, and dissociation in women with childhood abuse histories. *Journal of Consulting and Clinical Psychology, 74*(2), 219.

Straker, G. (1992). *Faces in the revolution: The psychological effects of violence on township youth in South Africa*. Cape Town, South Africa: David Philip.

Summerfield, D. (1997). The impact of war and atrocity on civilian populations: An overview of major themes. In H. Black, D. G. Nendricks, G. Mezey, & M. Newman (Eds.), *Psychological trauma: A developmental approach* (pp. 148-155). London, England: Royal College of Psychiatry.

Thabet, A. A. M., Vostanis, P., & Thabet, S. S. (2019). Impact of Trauma on Palestinian Children PTSD, Anxiety, Depression and Coping Strategies. *Current Trends in Medicine and Medical Research Vol. 1,* 4-23.

Thabet, A. A., & Vostanis, P. (1999). Post-traumatic stress reactions in children of war. *Journal of Child Psychology and Psychiatry and Allied Disciplines, 40*(3), 385-391.

Thabet, A. A., & Vostanis, P. (2000). Post-traumatic stress reactions in children of war: A longitudinal study. *Child Abuse Neglect, 24*, 291-298. doi:10.1016/S0145-2134(99)00127-1

Thabet, A. A., & Vostanis, P. (2011). Impact of political violence and trauma in Gaza on children's mental health and types of interventions: A review of research evidence in a historical context. *International Journal of Peace and Development Studies, 2*(8), 214-218.

Thabet, A. A., Tawahina, A. A., El Sarraj, E., & Vostanis, P. (2008). Exposure to war trauma and PTSD among parents and children in the Gaza strip. *European Child & Adolescent Psychiatry, 17*(4), 191. doi:10.1007/s00787-007-0653-9

Thabet, A. A., Vostanis, P., & Karim, K. (2015). Trauma exposure in pre-school children in a war zone. *British Journal of Psychiatry, 206*(2), 154-155.

The Dyregrov, Yehuda, R., Halligan, S. L., & Grossman, R. (2001).

Childhood trauma and risk for PTSD: Relationship to intergenerational effects of trauma, parental PTSD, and cortisol excretion. Development and Psychopathology, 13(3), 733-753.

Thulesius, H., & Håkansson, A. (1999). Screening for posttraumatic stress disorder symptoms among Bosnian refugees. *Journal of Traumatic Stress: Official Publication of the International Society for Traumatic Stress Studies, 12*(1), 167-174. doi:10.1023/A:1024758718971

UNICEF, "Gaza: 10 years, 10 facts," 2017.

UNICEF. (2005). *The state of the world's children 2006: Excluded and invisible.* New York, NY: Author.

UNICEF. (2014, September 8). *Treating the hidden wounds of Gaza's children.* Retrieved from https://www.unicef.org/mena/press-releases/treating-hidden-wounds-in-gaza

UNICEF. (2020). Children in war: Impact on the mental health and psychosocial well-being of children affected by armed conflict. Retrieved from https://data.unicef.org/resources/children-in-war/

United Against Torture (UAT) Coalition. (2009, April). *Israeli "Operation Cast Lead" - Gaza Strip (27 December 2008 - 18 January 2009): Supplementary Report For Consideration Regarding Israel's Fourth Periodic Report to the UN Committee Against Torture (CAT).* Retrieved from https://www2.ohchr.org/english/bodies/cat/docs/ngos/UATSupp_Israel42.pdf

United Nations Development Programme. (2015). *One year after Gaza early recovery and reconstruction needs assessment* (pp. 1-112, Rep.). Jerusalem, Israel: Author. doi:http://www.undp.ps/en/newsroom/publications/pdf/other/gazaoneyear.pdf

United Nations Office for the Coordination of Humanitarian Affairs (OCHA) (2015a, March 26). *Fragmented lives: Humanitarian overview 2014.* Retrieved from https://www.ochaopt.org/content/fragmented-lives-humanitarian-overview-2014

United Nations Office for the Coordination of Humanitarian Affairs (OCHA). (2015b, June 23). *Key figures on the 2014 hostilities.* Retrieved from https://www.ochaopt.org/content/key-figures-2014-hostilities#_ftn1

United Nations Office for the Coordination of Humanitarian Affairs (OCHA), "Gaza Emergency Situation Report," 2014.

United Nations Office for the Coordination of Humanitarian Affairs (OCHA). (2021). "Gaza Ten Years Later." https://www.ochaopt.org/content/gaza-ten-years-later

United Nations Relief and Works Agency for Palestine Refugees (UNRWA). (2015, September). *Gaza emergency UNRWA*. Retrieved from https://www.unrwa.org/gaza-emergency

United Nations Relief and Works Agency for Palestine Refugees in the Near East (UNRWA). (2021). "Gaza Situation Report." https://www.unrwa.org/resources/situation-report-gaza-strip-issue-70

United Nations. (1997, June 10). *Question of Palestine remains most intractable conflict situation in United Nations history. Meetings coverage and press releases*. Retrieved from https://www.un.org/press/en/1997/19970610.ga9250.html

United Nations. (2014a, August 22). *Hostilities in Gaza and Israel – OCHA situation report (22 August 2014) – Question of Palestine*. Retrieved from https://www.un.org/unispal/document/hostilities-in-gaza-and-israel-ocha-situation-report-22-august-2014/

United Nations. (2014b, October 9). *Gaza crisis appeal* (pp. 1-45, Rep.). East Jerusalem: Author. doi:https://unispal.un.org/pdfs/GazaCrisisAppeal_0914Update.pdf

UNRWA, "Gaza in 2020: A Livelihoods Perspective," 2021.

Weine, S., Becker, D. F., McGlashan, T. H., Vojvoda, D., Hartman, S., & Robbins, J. P. (1995). Adolescent survivors of "ethnic cleansing": Observations on the first year in America. *Journal of the American Academy of Child & Adolescent Psychiatry*, 34(9), 1153-1159. doi:10.1097/00004583-199509000-00012

Welbel, C. (2014, July 28). *No safe place for children in Gaza*. Retrieved from https://www.unicef.org/emergencies/oPt_74589.html

Werner, E. E. (1993). Risk, resilience, and recovery: Perspectives from the Kauai longitudinal study. *Development and Psychopathology*, 5(4), 503-515. doi:10.1017/S095457940000612X

Wessells, M. G. (1998). Children, armed conflict, and peace. *Journal of Peace Research*, *35*(5), 635-646. doi:10.1177/0022343398035005006

Winter, J. M. (2009). Sites of Memory, Sites of Mourning: The Great War in European Cultural History. Cambridge University Press.

World Food Programme (WFP), "Gaza Emergency Response Situation Report," 2021.

World Health Organization (WHO). (2001). *The world health report 2001: Mental health: New understanding, new hope.* Geneva, Switzerland: Author.

World Health Organization (WHO). (2014, August). *Gaza after the conflict: Assessing mental health needs.* Retrieved from http://www.emro.who.int/pse/palestine-infocus/gaza-after-the-conflict-assessing-mental-health-needs-august-2014.html

Wright, M. O'D., Masten, A. S., Northwood, A., & Hubbard, J. (1997). Long-term effects of massive trauma: Developmental and psychobiological perspectives. In D. Cicchetti & S. L. Toth (Eds.), *Rochester symposium on developmental psychopathology, Vol. 8., The effects of trauma on the developmental process* (pp. 181-225). Rochester, NY: University of Rochester Press.

Yablon, Y. B. (2001). Psychological implications of war and violence on children. International Review of Psychiatry, 13(1), 58-63.v.

Yehuda, R., Halligan, S. L., & Grossman, R. (2001). Childhood trauma and risk for PTSD: Relationship to intergenerational effects of trauma, parental PTSD, and cortisol excretion. Development and Psychopathology, 13(3), 733-753.

Yule, W. (2002). Alleviating the effects of war and displacement on children. *Traumatology*, *8*(3), 160. doi:10.1177/153476560200800304

Zahr, I. K. (1996). Effects of war on the behavior of Lebanese preschool children: Influence of home environment and family functioning. *American Journal of Orthopsychiatry*, *66*(3), 401-408. doi:0.1037/h0080190

Zivcic, I. (1993). Emotional reactions of children to war stress in Croatia. *Journal of the American Academy of Child & Adolescent Psychiatry*, *32*(4), 709-713. doi:10.1097/00004583-199307000-00002

Zonszein, M. (2015, March 27). Israel killed more Palestinians
    in 2014 than in any other year since 1967. *The Guardian*.
    Retrieved   from   https://www.theguardian.com/world/
    2015/mar/27/israel-kills-more-palestinians-2014-than-any-other-
    year-since-1967

الأطفال الفلسطينيون تحت الاحتلال | مركز المعلومات الوطني الفلسطيني
. (n.d.). Info.wafa.ps. Retrieved October 4, 2023, from https://info.wafa.
ps/ar_page.aspx?id=y7SojLa9133973541ay7SojL.

(Palestinian Health Ministry). (n.d.). Telegram. وزارة الصحة الفلسطينية
Retrieved December 3, 2023, from https://t.me/MOHMediaGaza/4506

About the Author

Iman Farajallah, PsyD, is a Doctor of Psychology practicing in the Bay Area, CA. She also holds an MA degree in Clinical Psychology from Sofia University, an MBS degree in International Relations from San Francisco State University, and other certificates. Dr. Farajallah is an adjunct professor at the Graduate Theological Union and Sofia University. Dr. Farajallah is the founder of Iman Network, a nonprofit organization that provides clinical treatment, education, and research to those who suffer from mental illnesses. Dr. Farajallah is an established researcher and writer and has recently published articles such as The Unseen Damage to Palestinian Children by the Israeli Occupation, War on Gaza: The Terrible Toll on Women's Mental and Physical Health, Palestinians are Raised in Survival Mode, but Nothing Prepared Us for this, coping with pandemics and positivity, the psychosocial impacts of war and armed conflict on Ukrainian children, and the psychological effects of the occupation and chronic warfare on Palestinian children. Dr. Farajallah also researches and develops treatments tailored to the specific needs of the Minority population. She provides training on PTSD and trauma. She is the producer and director of the film (Gaza's Children: Innocence Lost) and a soon-to-be-released film (My Life is a War: I Want to Live in Peace), which will be released in 2024.

www.ingramcontent.com/pod-product-compliance
Lightning Source LLC
Chambersburg PA
CBHW031506270326
41930CB00006B/273